Rowland Hill

A Collection of Psalms and Hymns

Chiefly Intended for the Use of the Poor

Rowland Hill

A Collection of Psalms and Hymns
Chiefly Intended for the Use of the Poor

ISBN/EAN: 9783744784917

Printed in Europe, USA, Canada, Australia, Japan

Cover: Foto ©Lupo / pixelio.de

More available books at **www.hansebooks.com**

A COLLECTION

OF

PSALMS AND HYMNS,

CHIEFLY INTENDED FOR

The Use of the POOR.

By ROWLAND HILL, M.A.
Chaplain to the Countess of CHESTERFIELD.

Let the Word of CHRIST dwell in you richly in all Wisdom; teaching and admonishing one another in Psalms, and Hymns, and spiritual Songs: singing with Grace in your Hearts unto the LORD, *Col.* i. 16.

Sing ye Praises with Understanding, *Psal.* xlvii. 7.

LONDON:

Printed in the Year M DCC LXXIV.

COURTEOUS READER,

NOTHING but a Desire of serving the Poor could have influenced me to have added to the Number of the many and excellent Collections of HYMNS, we have already in Use amongst us; but as many of them are now swollen far beyond their original Size, and consequently the Prices raised much higher than the generality of the Poor can reach, I thought an Extract of those HYMNS which are mostly in Use, might not be unserviceable. A very few new ones, however, have I ventured to add, upon some particular Subjects, where they seemed to be wanting. And as modest Words before GOD become us best, those HYMNS which favoured of an unmeaning Moravian Stile, or of the self-confident Language of the Free-willer, have I ventured, here and there, a little to alter. And that there might be a few upon every Subject, and those easily found out, I have placed them in the following Order:— Morning Hymns — Evening Hymns — Hymns for the Lord's Day — Hymns for opening Public Worship — Before Sermon — After Sermon — Before or After Sermon — Invitation Hymns — General Hymns of Prayer — General Hymns of Praise — Festival Hymns — Funeral Hymns — Judgment Hymns — Hymns for Ministers — Hymns at Meeting and Parting, &c. — Hymns for Baptism and the Lord's Supper — Dismission Hymns, and Doxologies. "*Much in a little*," is what GOD gives us in his Word:—This I have aimed at in this little Collection. That GOD may give us to sing his Praises with the Understanding and the Heart, is the sincere Prayer of,

Thine for CHRIST's Sake,

A COLLECTION
OF
PSALMS and HYMNS.

MORNING HYMNS.

HYMN I.

JESUS the all-restoring Word,
  Our fallen Spirit's Hope,
After thy lovely Likeness, LORD,
  O when shall we wake up!

Thou, O our GOD, Thou only art
  The Life, the Truth, the Way;
Quicken our Souls, instruct our Hearts,
  Our sinking Footsteps stay.

All that Thou dost on Earth bestow,
  Or Heaven, vouchsafe to give;
Give us, O LORD Thyself to know,
  In Thee to walk and live.

Fill us with all the Life of Love:
  In mystic Union join
Us to Thyself; and let us prove
  Sweet Fellowship divine.

B

HYMN II. *The same.*

RISE, my Soul! adore thy Maker,
   Angels Praise, join thy Lays,
With them be Partaker.

FATHER, LORD of ev'ry Spirit!
   In thy Light lead me right,
Thro' my SAVIOUR's Merit.

Thou this Night waſt my Protector,
   With me ſtay all the Day,
Ever my Director.

Holy, Holy, Holy Giver
   Of all Good, Life and Food,
Reign ador'd for ever.

Glory, Honour, Thanks, and Bleſſing,
   Give we Thee, One in Three,
Never, never ceaſing.

EVENING HYMNS.

HYMN III.

JESUS, the all-atoning Lamb,
   Lover of loſt Mankind;
Salvation in whoſe only Name
   A ſinful World can find;

We aſk thy Grace to make us clean;
   We come to Thee, our GOD;
Open, O LORD, for this Day's Sin,
   The Fountain of thy Blood.

Hither our ſinful Souls be brought,
   And ev'ry idle Word,
And ev'ry Work, and ev'ry Thought,
   That hath not pleas'd our LORD.

Hither our Actions, righteous deem'd
  By Man, and counted Good,
As filthy Rags by God esteem'd,
  Till sprinkled with thy Blood.

To Thee then O vouchsafe us Power
  For Pardon still to flee;
And every Day, and every Hour,
  To wash ourselves in Thee.

HYMN IV. *The same*

ERE I sleep, for ev'ry Favor
  This Day shewed by my God,
I will bless my Saviour.

O my Lord, what shall I render
  To Thy Name, still the same,
Gracious, good, and tender?

Leave me not, but ever love me:
  Let thy Peace be my Bliss,
Till thou hence remove me.

Visit me with thy Salvation;
  Let thy Care now be near,
Round my Habitation.

Thou, my Rock, my Guard, my Tower,
  Safely keep, while I Sleep,
Me with all thy Power.

So whene'er in Death I slumber
  Let me rise with the Wise,
Counted in their Number.

HYMN V.
Morning or Evening.

O God, how endless is thy Love,
  Thy Gifts are ev'ry Ev'ning new;
And Morning Mercies, from above,
  Gently distil like early Dew.

Thou spread'st the Curtain of the Night,
  Great Guardian of our sleeping Hours;
Thy sov'reign Word restores the Light,
  And quickens all our drowsy Pow'rs.

We yield our Pow'rs to thy Command,
  To thee we consecrate our Days;
Perpetual Blessings from thine Hand
  Demand perpetual Songs of Praise.

HYMN VI.
Hymns for the Lord's Day.

SWEET is the Work, O God, our King,
  To praise thy Name, give Thanks, and sing:
To shew thy Love by Morning Light,
And talk of all thy Truth by Night.

Sweet is the Day of sacred Rest,
No mortal Care should seize our Breast;
O may our Hearts in Tune be found,
Like David's Harp of solemn Sound!

Our Hearts should triumph in thee, Lord,
And bless thy Work, and bless thy Word;
Thy Works of Grace, how bright they shine!
How deep thy Counsels! how divine!

O may we see, and hear, and know,
What Mortals cannot reach below:
May all our Pow'rs find sweet Employ
In Christ's eternal World of Joy.

HYMN VII. *The same.*

1 WELCOME sweet Day of Rest,
    That saw the LORD arise;
Welcome to the rising Breast,
    And these rejoicing Eyes!

The King himself comes near,
    And feasts his Saints to-day;
Here we may sit, and see him here,
    And love, and praise, and pray.

One Day amidst the Place
    Where my dear GOD hath been,
Is sweeter than ten thousand Days
    Of pleasurable Sin.

My willing Soul would stay
    In such a Frame as this,
And sit and sing herself away
    To everlasting Bliss.

HYMN VIII. *The same.*
Hosanna in the Highest.

THIS is the Day the LORD hath made,
    He calls the Hours his own;
Let Heav'n rejoice, let Earth be glad,
    And Praise surround the Throne.

To-day CHRIST rose, and left the Dead,
    And Satan's Empire fell;
To-day the Saints his Triumphs spread,
    And all his Wonders tell.

Hosanna to th' anointed King,
  To David's holy Son:
Hosanna's loud to Thee we sing,
  Like those around the Throne.

Hosanna, let the Earth and Skies
  Repeat the joyful Sound;
Rocks, Hills and Vales reflect the Voice,
  In one eternal Round.

Hosanna, in the highest Strain
  The Church on Earth can raise!
The highest Heav'ns in which he reigns
  Shall give him nobler Praise.

HYMN IX.

Opening Public Worship.

NOW may the Spirit's Holy Fire,
  Descending from above,
His waiting Family inspire
  With Joy, and Peace, and Love!

Thee we the Comforter confess:
  Unless thou'rt present here,
Our Songs of Praise are vain Address,
  We utter heartless Pray'r.

Wake, heav'nly Wind, arise and come,
  Blow on the drooping Field;
Our Spices then shall breathe Perfume,
  And fragrant Incense yield.

Touch, with a living Coal, the Lip
  That shall proclaim thy Word,
And bid each awful Hearer keep
  Attention to the LORD.

Haften the Reftitution Day;
  Thy Pow'r we wait to prove:
Thy glorious Grace to each difplay,
  And fill our Souls with Love.

HYMN X. *The fame.*

FAR from our Thoughts vain World begone,
  Let our religious Hours alone;
O may our Eyes our Saviour fee!
We wait a Vifit, LORD, from thee.

O warm our Hearts with holy Fire,
And kindle there a pure Defire,
Come, our Dear JESUS, from above,
And feed our Souls with heav'nly Love.

The Trees of Life immortal ftand
In fragrant Rows at thy right Hand;
And in fweet Murmurs by their Side
Rivers of Blifs perpetual glide.

Hafte then, and with a fmiling Face,
Come, fpread the Tables of thy Grace:
Bring down a Tafte of Truth divine,
And chear our Hearts with facred Wine.

Bleft JESUS, what delicious Fare!
How fweet thy Entertainments are!
Never did Angels tafte above
Redeeming Grace and dying Love.

Hail, great Emmanuel, all Divine!
In thee thy Father's Glories fhine:
Thou brighteft, fweeteft, faireft one,
That Eyes have feen, or Angels known!

HYMN XI. *The same.*

LORD, we come before thee now,
At thy Feet we humbly bow;
Oh! do not our Suit disdain:
Shall we seek thee, LORD, in vain?
LORD, on thee our Souls depend;
In Compassion now descend;
Fill our Hearts with thy rich Grace,
Tune our Lips to sing thy Praise.

In thine own appointed Way,
Now we seek thee; here we stay;
LORD, we know not how to go,
Till a Blessing thou bestow;
Send some Message from thy Word,
That may Joy and Peace afford;
Let thy Spirit now impart
Full Salvation to each Heart.

Comfort those who weep and mourn,
Let the Time of Joy return;
Those that are cast down lift up,
Make them strong in Faith and Hope;
Grant that those who seek may find
Thee a GOD divinely kind:
Heal the Sick, the Captive free:
Let us all rejoice in Thee.

HYMN XII.
Before Sermon.

NOW begin the heav'nly Theme,
Sing aloud in JESU's Name,
Ye who JESU's Kindness prove,
Triumph in redeeming Love.

Ye who see the Father's Grace,
Beaming in the Saviour's Face,
As to Canaan on ye move,
Praise and bless redeeming Love.

Mourning Souls, dry up your Tears,
Banish all your guilty Fears;
See your Guilt and Curse remove,
Cancell'd by redeeming Love.

Ye, alas! who long have been
Willing Slaves of Death and Sin,
Now from Bliss no longer rove,
Stop and taste redeeming Love.

Welcome all by Sin oppress'd,
Welcome to his sacred Rest,
Nothing brought Him from above,
Nothing but redeeming Love.

He subdu'd th' infernal Pow'rs,
Those tremendous Foes of ours;
From their cursed Empire drove,
Mighty in redeeming Love.

HYMN XIII. *The same.*

LET ev'ry mortal Ear attend,
   And ev'ry Heart rejoice,
The Trumpet of the GOSPEL sounds
   With an inviting Voice.

Ho! all ye hungry starving Souls,
   That feed upon the Wind,
And vainly strive with earthly Toys
   To fill an empty Mind:

Eternal Wisdom hath prepar'd
   A Soul-reviving Feast,
And bids our longing Appetites
   The rich Provision taste.

Ho! ye that pant for living Streams,
   And pine away and die,
Here you may quench your raging Thirst
   With springs that never dry.

Dear God, the Treasures of thy Love,
   Are everlasting Mines,
Deep as our helpless Mis'ries are,
   And boundless as our Sins.

The happy Gates of GOSPEL-GRACE,
   Stand open Night and Day;
Lord, we are come to seek Supplies
   And drive our Wants away.

HYMN XIV. *The same.*

BLOW ye the Trumpet, blow
   The gladly solemn Sound,
Let all the Nations know
   To Earth's remotest Bound.
The Year of Jubilee is come;
Return, ye ransom'd Sinners, home!

The Gospel Trumpet hear,
   The News of heav'nly Grace;
Ye happy Souls draw near,
   Behold your SAVIOUR'S Face:
The Year of Jubilee is come;
Return to your eternal Home.

Extol the Lamb of God,
　The all-atoning Lamb;
Redemption in his Blood
　Throughout the World proclaim:
The Year of Jubilee is come:
Return, ye ransom'd Sinners, home!

HYMN XV.
Before or after Sermon.

BLEST are the Souls that hear and know
　The Gospel's joyful Sound;
Peace shall attend the Path they go,
　And Light their Steps surround.

Their Joy shall bear their Spirits up,
　Thro' their Redeemer's Name!
His Righteousness exalts their Hope;
　Nor Satan dares condemn.

The LORD, our Glory and Defence,
　Strength and Salvation gives;
Israel, thy King for ever reigns,
　Thy GOD for ever lives

HYMN XVI. *The same.*

SALVATION, O the joyful Sound,
　What Pleasure to our Ears!
A sov'reign Balm for ev'ry Wound,
　A Cordial for our Fears.

Bury'd in Sorrow, and in Sin,
　At Hell's dark Door we lay!
O may we rise by Grace divine,
　To see a heav'nly Day!

Salvation! let the Echo fly
  The spacious Earth around,
While all the Armies of the Sky
  Conspire to raise the Sound.

HYMN XVII. *The same.*

PRAISE ye the Lord, exalt his Name,
    While in his holy Courts ye wait;
Ye Saints, that to his House belong,
Or stand attending at his Gate.

Praise ye the Lord; the Lord is good:
To praise his Name is sweet Employ;
Isr'el he chose of old, and still
His Church is his peculiar Joy.

Bless ye the Lord, who taste his Love:
People and Priests exalt his Name;
Amongst his Saints he ever dwells,
His Church is his Jerusalem.

HYMN XVIII. *The same.*

YE that in his Courts are found,
    List'ning to the joyful Sound,
Lost and helpless as ye are,
Sons of Sorrow, Sin, and Care,
Glorify the King of Kings,
Take the Peace the Gospel brings.

Turn to Christ your longing Eyes,
View his bloody Sacrifice;
See in Him your Sins forgiv'n,
Pardon, Holiness, and Heav'n:
Glorify the King of Kings,
Take the Peace the Gospel brings.

INVITATION HYMNS.
HYMN XIX.

SINNERS, obey the Gospel-Word,
Haste to the Supper of your LORD,
Be wise to know your gracious Day,
All Things are ready, come away!

Ready the Father is to own,
And kiss his late-returning Son;
Ready the loving SAVIOUR stands,
And spreads for you his bleeding Hands.

Ready the Spirit of his Love,
Just now the stony Heart to move;
T' apply and witness with the Blood,
And wash and seal you Sons of GOD.

Ready for you the Angels wait,
To triumph in your blest Estate:
Tuning their Harps, they long to praise
The Wonders of redeeming Grace.

Come then, ye Sinners, to your LORD,
To Happiness in CHRIST restor'd;
His proffer'd Benefits embrace,
And freely now be sav'd by Grace.

HYMN XX. *The same.*

COME, ye Sinners, poor and wretched,
Weak and wounded, sick and sore;
JESUS ready stands to save you,
  Full of Pity join'd with Pow'r.
He is able, &c.
  He is willing: doubt no more.

Ho! ye needy; come, and welcome;
   God's free Bounty glorify.
True Belief, and true Repentance,
   Every Grace that brings us nigh;
Without Money, &c.
   Come to Jesus Christ, and buy.

Let not Conscience make you linger;
   Nor of Fitness fondly dream:
All the Fitness he requireth
   Is, to feel your Need of Him.
This he gives you, &c.
   'Tis the Spirit's rising Beam.

Come, ye weary, heavy laden,
   Bruis'd and mangled by the Fall;
If you tarry till you're better,
   You will never come at all.
Not the Righteous, &c.
   Sinners, Jesus came to call.

Agonizing in the Garden,
   Lo! your Maker prostrate lies;
On the bloody Tree behold him:
   Hear him cry, before he dies,
It is finish'd; &c.
   Sinners, will not this suffice?

Lo! th' incarnate God, ascended,
   Pleads the Merit of his Blood.
Venture on him, venture wholly;
   Let no other Trust intrude.
None but Jesus, &c.
   Can do helpless Sinners good.

Saints and Angels join'd in Concert,
   Sing the Praises of the LAMB;
While the blissful Seats to Heav'n
   Sweetly echo with his Name.
Hallelujah! &c.
   Sinners here may sing the same.

HYMN XXI. *The same.*

HIther ye Poor, ye Sick, ye Blind,
   A sin-disorder'd, trembling Throng:
To you the Gospel calls, to you
   MESSIAH's Blessings all belong.

The Sons of Reason and of Pride,
   Reject the Blessings of his Tree:
For Sinners only JESUS dy'd;
   Sinner behold! He dy'd for Thee.

'Twas with our Griefs MESSIAH groan'd;
   'Twas with our Guilt his Soul was try'd
Our Punishment he took, he bore;
   And Sinners liv'd when JESUS dy'd!

Awake each Heart, arise each Soul,
   And join the blissful Choirs above:
May nothing tune our future Song.
   But heav'nly Wisdom, heav'nly Love!

HYMN XXII.
After Sermon.

NOW to the Pow'r of GOD supreme,
   Be everlasting Honours giv'n;
He saves from Hell, (we bless his Name)
He calls lost wand'ring Souls to Heav'n.

Not for our Duties or Deserts,
But of his own abounding Grace,
He works Salvation in our Hearts,
And forms a People for his Praise.

'Twas his own Purpose that begun
To rescue Rebels doom'd to die;
He gave us Grace in CHRIST his Son,
Before he spread the starry Sky.

JESUS, the LORD, appears at last,
And makes his Father's Counsels known:
Declares the great Transactions past,
And brings immortal Blessings down.

HYMN XXIII. *The same.*

FROM all that dwell below the Skies,
    Let the Creator's Praise arise;
Let the Redeemer's Name be sung
Thro' ev'ry Land, by ev'ry Tongue.

Eternal are thy Mercies, LORD:
Eternal Truth attends thy Word;
Thy Praise shall sound from Shore to Shore,
Till Suns shall rise and set no more.

HYMN XXIV.

COME, guilty Souls, and fly away
    To CHRIST, and heal your Wounds;
This is the welcome GOSPEL-Day,
    Wherein free Grace abounds.

GOD lov'd the World, and gave his Son
    To drink the Cup of Wrath:
And JESUS says, he'll cast out none
    That come to him by Faith.

HYMN XXV. *The same.*

O JESU our LORD,
   Thy Name be ador'd,
For all the rich Bleſſings convey'd thro' thy Word.

   In Spirit we trace
   Thy Wonders of Grace,
And chearfully join in a Concert of Praiſe.

   The Ancient of Days
   His Glory diſplays,
And ſhines on his Choſen with cheriſhing Rays.

   The Trumpet of GOD
   Is ſounding abroad,
The Language of Mercy, Salvation thro' Blood.

   Thrice happy are they
   Who hear and obey,
And ſhare in the Bleſſings of this Goſpel-Day.

   The People who know
   The Saviour below,
With burning Affection to worſhip him glow.

   This Bleſſing be mine,
   Through Favour divine;
But, O my Redeemer, the Glory be thine.

   The Work is of Grace,
   Thine, thine, be the Praiſe,
And mine to adore Thee and tell of thy Ways.

HYMN XXVI.

LADEN with Guilt, Sinners ariſe,
   And view your bleeding Sacrifice;
Each purple Drop proclaims there's Room,
And bids the Poor and Needy come!

Beneath your Crimes the Victim stood,
Sign'd your Acquittances in Blood;
Hereby stern Justice is appeas'd:
Sinners, look up, and be releas'd!

Mercy, Truth, Peace, and Righteousness,
Beam from the Reconciler's Face;
Here look, till Love dissolves your Heart,
And bids your slavish Fears depart.

Oh! quit the World's delusive Charms,
And quickly fly to JESU's Arms;
Wrestle until your GOD is known,
Till you can call the LORD your own.

HYMN XXVII.

General Hymns of Prayer and Praise.

Hymns of Prayer.

O Come, thou wounded Lamb of GOD,
   Come, wash us in thy cleansing Blood;
Give us to know thy Love, then Pain
Is sweet, and Life or Death is Gain.

Take our poor Hearts, and let them be
For ever clos'd to all but Thee:
Seal Thou our Breasts, and let us wear
That Pledge of Love for ever there.

How can it be, thou heav'nly King,
That thou should'st Man to Glory bring!
Make Slaves the Partners of thy Throne,
Deck'd with a never-fading Crown!

Ah, LORD! enlarge our scanty Thought,
To know the Wonders thou hast wrought;
Unloose our stamm'ring Tongue to tell
Thy Love immense, unsearchable.

Firstborn of many Brethren Thou,
To Thee both Earth and Heav'n must bow;
Help us to Thee our All to give:
Thine may we die, thine may we live!

HYMN XXVIII.

O Lord, how great's the Favour!
   That we, such Sinners poor,
Can thro' thy Blood's sweet Savour
   Approach thy Mercy's Door,
And find an open Passage
   Unto the Throne of Grace;
There wait the welcome Message
   That bids us go in Peace?

Lord, we are helpless Creatures,
   Full of the deepest Need;
Throughout defil'd by Nature,
   Stupid, and inly dead:
Our Strength is perfect Weakness,
   And all we have is Sin:
Our Hearts are all Uncleanness,
   A Den of Thieves within.

In this forlorn Condition,
   Who shall afford us Aid!
Where shall we find Compassion,
   But in the Church's Head?
Jesus, thou art all Pity,
   Oh take us to thine Arms,
And exercise thy Mercy,
   To save us from all Harms.

We'll never cease repeating,
   Our numberless Complaints,
But ever be intreating
   The glorious King of Saints:
Till we attain the Image
   Of Him we inly love,
And pay our grateful Homage
   With all the Saints above.

Then we, with all in Glory,
   Shall thankfully relate
Th' amazing pleasing Story,
   Of Jesu's Love so great:
In this blest Contemplation
   We shall for ever dwell,
And prove such Consolation
   As none below can tell.

HYMN XXIX.

JESUS, lover of my Soul,
   Let me to thy Bosom fly,
While the nearer Waters roll,
   While the Tempest still is high;
Hide me, O my Saviour, hide,
   Till the Storm of Life is past:
Safe into the Haven guide;
   O receive my Soul at last!

Other Refuge have I none:
   Hangs my helpless Soul on Thee?
Leave, ah! leave me not alone,
   Still support and comfort me:
All my Trust on Thee is stay'd,
   . All mine Help from Thee I bring;
Cover my defenceless Head
   With the Shadow of thy Wing.

Thou, O CHRIST, art all I want;
  More than All in Thee I find:
Raise the Fallen, chear the Faint,
  Heal the Sick, and lead the Blind.
Just and holy is thy Name,
  I am all Unrighteousness!
Vile and full of Sin I am:
  Thou art full of Truth and Grace.
Plenteous Grace with Thee is found,
  Grace to pardon all my Sin:
Let the healing Streams abound;
  Make, and keep me pure within:
Thou of Life the Fountain art,
  Freely let me take of Thee:
Spring Thou up within mine Heart,
  Rise to all Eternity!

HYMN XXX.

SON of GOD! thy Blessing grant,
  Still supply my ev'ry Want:
Tree of Life, thine Influence shed,
With thy Sap my Spirit feed!

Tend'rest Branch, alas! am I,
Wither without Thee, and die:
Weak as helpless Infancy;
O confirm my Soul in Thee!

Unsustain'd by Thee, I fall:
Send the Strength for which I call!
Weaker than a bruised Reed,
Help I every Moment need.

All my Hopes on Thee depend:
Love me! save me to the End!
Give me the continuing Grace:
Take the everlasting Praise!

HYMN XXXI.

LORD, we are vile, conceiv'd in Sin,
  And born unholy and unclean;
Sprung from the Man whose guilty Fall
Corrupts the Race, and taints us all.

Soon as we draw our Infant Breath,
The Seeds of Sin grow up for Death!
Thy Law demands a perfect Heart,
But we're defil'd in ev'ry Part.

Behold! we fall before thy Face:
Our only Refuge is thy Grace.
No outward Forms can make us clean,
The Leprosy lies deep within.

JESUS, our GOD! thy Blood alone
Hath Pow'r sufficient to atone;
LORD! let us hear thy pard'ning Voice,
And make our down-cast Hearts rejoice!

HYMN XXXII.

HE dies! the FRIEND of Sinners dies!
  Lo! Salem's Daughters weep around!
A solemn Darkness veils the Skies!
  A sudden Trembling shakes the Ground!
Come Saints, and drop a Tear or two,
  For Him who groan'd beneath your Load;
He shed a thousand Drops for you,
  A thousand Drops of richer Blood!

Here's Love and Grief beyond Degree;
 -The LORD of Glory dies for Men!
But lo! what sudden Joys we see!
 JESUS the Dead revives again!
The rising GOD forsakes the Tomb!
 (The Tomb in vain forbids his Rise!)
Cherubic Legions guard him home,
 And shout Him welcome to the Skies!

Break off your Tears, ye Saints! and tell
 How high our great Deliv'rer reigns!
Sing how He spoil'd the Hosts of Hell,
 And led the Monster Death in Chains!
Say "Live for ever, wond'rous King!
 "Born to redeem! and strong to save:"
Then ask the Monster---"Where's thy Sting?
 "And where's thy Victory, boasting Grave!"

HYMN XXXIII.

HOLY Lamb, who thee receive,
 Who in thee begin to live:
Day and Night they cry to thee;
As thou art, so let us be.

Fix, O fix each wav'ring Mind,
To thy Cross our Spirits bind;
Earthly Passions far remove,
Swallow up our Souls in Love.

Dust and Ashes tho' we be,
Full of Guilt and Misery:
Thine we are, thou Son of GOD;
Take the Purchase of thy Blood.

Boundless Wisdom, Pow'r divine,
Love unspeakable, are thine;
Praise by all to Thee be giv'n,
Sons of Earth and Hosts of Heav'n.

HYMN XXXIV.

COME, dearest Lord, descend and dwell,
By Faith, and Love, in ev'ry Breast;
Then shall we know, and taste, and feel,
The Joys that cannot be express'd.

Come, fill our Hearts with inward Strength;
Make our enlarged Souls possess,
And learn the Height, and Breadth, and Length
Of thine unmeasurable Grace.

Now to the God whose Pow'r can do
More than our Thoughts or Wishes know,
Be everlasting Honours done,
By all the Church, through Christ his Son!

HYMN XXXV.

NOT all the Blood of Beasts
On Jewish Altars slain,
Could give the guilty Conscience Peace,
Or wash away the Stain.

But Christ, the heav'nly Lamb,
Takes all our Sins away;
A Sacrifice of nobler Name,
And richer Blood than they.

My Faith would lay her Hand
On that dear Head of thine,
While like a Penitent I stand,
And there confess my Sin.

My Soul looks back to see
The Burdens thou didst bear,
When hanging on the cursed Tree;
And hopes her Guilt was there. Be

Believing, we rejoice
  To see the Curse remove;
We bless the Lamb with chearful Voice,
  And sing his bleeding Love.

HYMN XXXVI.

WITH Joy we meditate the Grace
  Of our High Priest above;
His Heart is made of Tenderness,
  His Bowels melt with Love.

Touch'd with a Sympathy within,
  He knows our feeble Frame;
He knows what sore Temptations mean,
  For he hath felt the same.

He in the Days of feeble Flesh,
  Pour'd out his Cries and Tears:
And in his Measure feels afresh,
  What ev'ry Member bears.

He'll never quench the smoaking Flax,
  But raise it to a Flame:
The bruised Reed He never breaks,
  Nor scorns the meanest Name.

Then, let our humble Faith address
  His Mercy and his Pow'r;
We shall obtain deliv'ring Grace
  In the distressing Hour.

HYMN XXXVII.

O Patient, spotless Lamb!
  My Heart in Patience keep,
To bear the Cross, so easy made,
  By wounding Thee so deep.

Bring me, my Shepherd, where
   Thy choicest Flocks abide;
From wand'ring save my foolish Heart,
   And keep it near thy Side.

My Friend, thou hast enough
   My Mis'ry to relieve:
Tho' Sin and Guilt oppress me sore,
   The Balm is thine to give.

Do Thou, my ALL, unite
   My Heart so firm to Thee,
That ev'ry where, and at all Times,
   Thy Love my ALL may be.

HYMN XXXVIII.

THOU hidden Love of GOD, whose Heig,
   Whose Depth unfathom'd no Man knows,
I see from far thy beauteous Light;
Inly I sigh for thy Repose.
My Heart is pain'd, nor can it be
At rest, till it finds Rest in thee.

Is there a Thing beneath the Sun
That strives with thee my Heart to share?
Ah tear it thence, and reign alone,
The LORD of ev'ry Motion there:
Then shall my Heart from Earth be free,
When it has found Repose in thee.

O hide this Self from me, that I
No more, but CHRIST in me may live:
My vile Affections crucify,
Nor let one darling Lust survive.
In all Things nothing may I see,
Nothing desire, or seek but thee.

Love, thy fov'reign Aid impart,
Save me from low-thoughted Care:
Chase this Self-will through all my Heart,
Through all its latent Mazes there:
Make me thy duteous Child, that I
Ceafelefs may 'Abba, Father, cry.

Each Moment draw from Earth away
My Heart, that lowly waits thy Call;
Speak to my inmoft Soul, and fay,
I am thy Love, thy God, thy All!
To feel thy Pow'r, to hear thy Voice,
To tafte thy Love, be all my Choice.

HYMN XXXIX.

PLUNG'D in a Gulph of dark Defpair
   We wretched Sinners lay,
Without one chearful Beam of Hope,
Or Spark of glimm'ring Day.

With pitying Eyes, the Prince of Grace
Beheld our helplefs Grief;
He faw, and (O amazing Love!)
He came to our Relief.

Down from the fhining Seats above,
With joyful Hafte he fled,
Enter'd the Grave in mortal Flefh,
And dwelt among the Dead.

O! for this Love let Rocks and Hills
Their lafting Silence break,
And all harmonious human Tongues,
The Saviour's Praifes fpeak!

Angels affift our mighty Joys,
Strike all your Harps of Gold;
But when you raife your higheft Notes,
His Love can ne'er be told!

HYMN XL.

LORD, take my Heart juft as it is,
   Set up therein thy Throne;
So shall I love Thee above all,
   And live to Thee alone.

Complete thy Work, and crown thy Grace,
   That I may faithful prove,
And liften to that fmall ftill Voice,
   Which only whifpers Love.

Which teaches me what is thy Will,
   And tells me what to do;
Which covers me with Shame, when I
   Do not thy Will purfue.

This Unction may I ever feel,
   This Teaching from my LORD,
And learn Obedience to thy Voice,
   Thy foft reviving Word.

HYMN XLI.

LONG have we fat beneath the Sound
   Of thy Salvation, LORD;
But ftill how weak our Faith is found,
   And Knowledge of thy Word!

Oft we frequent thine holy Place,
   Yet hear almoft in vain:
How fmall a Portion of thy Grace
   Do our falfe Hearts retain!

Our gracious SAVIOUR and our GOD!
   How little art Thou known,
By all the Judgments of thy Rod,
   And Bleffings of thy Throne?

How cold and feeble is our Love!
　　How negligent our Fear!
How low our Hope of Joys above!
　　How few Affections there!

Great God! thy sov'reign Aid impart,
　　To give thy Word Success;
Write thy Salvation on each Heart,
　　And make us learn thy Grace.

Shew our forgetful Feet the Way
　　That leads to Joys on high;
Where Knowledge grows without Decay,
　　And Love shall never die.

HYMN XLII.

HOW heavy is the Night,
　　That hangs upon our Eyes,
'Till CHRIST with his reviving Light
　　Over our Souls arise!

Our guilty Spirits dread
　　To meet the Wrath of Heav'n:
But in his Righteousness array'd,
　　We see our Sins forgiv'n.

Unholy and impure
　　Are all our Thoughts and Ways;
His Hands infected Nature cure,
　　With sanctifying Grace.

The Pow'rs of Hell agree
　　To hold our Souls in vain;
He sets the Sons of Bondage free,
　　And breaks the cursed Chain.

Lord, we adore thy Ways
That bring us near to God:
Thy sov'reign Pow'r, thy healing Grace,
And thine atoning Blood!

HYMN XLIII.

WHY should the Children of a King
    Go mourning all their Days?
Great Comforter! descend, and bring
    Some Tokens of thy Grace.

Dost thou not dwell in all thy Saints,
    And seal the Heirs of Heav'n?
When wilt thou banish their Complaints,
    And shew their Sins forgiv'n?

Assure each Conscience of its Part
    In the Redeemer's Blood,
And bear thy Witness in each Heart,
    That it is born of God.

Thou art the Earnest of his Love,
    The Pledge of Joys to come;
May thy blest Wings, celestial Dove!
    Safely convey us home.

HYMN XLIV.

COME, holy Spirit, heav'nly Dove,
    With all thy quick'ning Pow'rs,
Kindle a Flame of sacred Love
    In these cold Hearts of ours.

Look how we grovel here below,
    Fond of these earthly Toys;
Our Souls how heavily they go
    To reach eternal Joys!

In vain we tune our formal Songs,
   In vain we strive to rise;
Hosannas languish on our Tongues,
   And our Devotion dies.

Dear Lord! and shall we ever live
   At this poor dying Rate;
Our Love so faint, so cold to Thee,
   And thine to us so great?

Come, holy Spirit, heav'nly Dove,
   With all thy quick'ning Pow'rs;
Come, shed abroad a Saviour's Love,
   And that shall kindle ours.

HYMN XLV.

THOU Shepherd of Isr'el divine,
   The Joy of the Upright in Heart,
For closer Communion they pine,
Still, still to reside where thou art;
The Pasture, Oh! when shall we find,
Where all, who their Shepherd obey,
Are fed on thy Bosom reclin'd,
Are skreen'd from the Heat of the Day.

Ah, shew us that happiest Place,
That Place of thy People's Abode,
Where Saints in an Extasy gaze,
And hang on a crucify'd GOD:
Thy Love for lost Sinners declare,
Thy Passion and Death on the Tree;
Our Spirits to Calvary bear,
To suffer and triumph with thee.

'Tis there with the Lambs of thy Flock,
There only we'd covet to rest,
To lie at the Foot of the Rock,
Or rise to be hid in thy Breast;
'Tis there we wou'd always abide,
And never a Moment depart,
Preserv'd evermore by thy Side,
Eternally hid in thine Heart.

HYMN XLVI.

AND are we Wretches yet alive?
   And do we yet rebel!
'Tis boundless, 'tis amazing Love,
   That bears us up from Hell.

The Burden of our weighty Guilt
   Would sink us down to Flames,
And threat'ning Vengeance rolls above,
   To crush our feeble Frames.

Almighty Goodness cries, Forbear,
   And strait the Thunder stays;
And dare we now provoke his Wrath,
   And weary out his Grace?

Lord, we have long abus'd thy Love,
   Too long indulg'd our Sin;
O that our Hearts may bleed, to see
   What Rebels we have been!

No more, our Lusts, may ye command,
   No more may we obey!
Stretch out, O GOD, thy conqu'ring Hand,
   And drive thy Foes away.

HYMN XLVII.

MY God, my Life, my Love,
   To Thee, to Thee I call,
I cannot live if thou remove,
   For thou art All in All.

Thy shining Grace can cheer
   This Dungeon where I dwell;
'Tis Paradise when thou art here;
   If thou depart, 'tis Hell.

The Smilings of thy Face,
   How amiable they are!
'Tis Heav'n to rest in thine Embrace,
   And no where else but there.

To Thee, and Thee alone,
   The Angels owe their Bliss;
They sit around thy gracious Throne,
   And dwell where JESUS is.

Not all the Harps above
   Can make a heav'nly Place,
If GOD his Residence remove,
   Or but conceal his Face:

Nor Earth, nor all the Sky,
   Can one Delight afford;
No, not a Drop of real Joy,
   Without thy Presence LORD.

Thou art the Sea of Love
   Where all my Pleasures roll,
The Circle where my Passions move,
   And Centre of my Soul.

HYMN XLVIII.

Isaiah IX. 2.

LIGHT of thofe whofe dreary Dwelling
  Borders on the Shades of Death,
Come! and by thy Love's revealing,
  Diffipate the Clouds beneath:
The new Heav'n and Earth's Creator,
  In our deepeft Darknefs rife!
Scatt'ring all the Night of Nature,
  Pouring Eye-fight on our Eyes!

Still we wait for thine Appearing,
  Life and Joy thy Beams impart;
Chafing all our Fears, and chearing
  Ev'ry poor benighted Heart:
Come, and manifeft the Favour
  Thou haft for the ranfom'd Race;
Come, thou dear exalted Saviour,
  Come, and bring thy Gofpel-grace.

Save us in thy great Compaffion,
  O thou mild pacific Prince!
Give the Knowledge of Salvation,
  Give the Pardon of our Sins!
By thine all-reftoring Merit,
  Ev'ry burden'd Soul releafe;
Ev'ry weary, wand'ring fpirit
  Guide into thy perfect Peace.

HYMN XLIX.

LORD, if thou the Grace impart,
  Poor in Spirit, Meek in Heart,
I shall as my Master be,
Rooted in Humility.

From the Time that Thee I knew,
Nothing wou'd I have in view;
Aim at nothing Great or High,
Lowly both in Heart and Eye.

Simple, Teachable, and Mild,
Chang'd into a little Child;
Pleas'd with all the LORD provides,
Wean'd from all the World besides.

Father, fix my Soul on Thee;
Ev'ry Evil let me flee;
Nothing want beneath, above,
Happy in thy precious Love.

O! that all may seek, and find
Every Good in JESUS join'd!
Him let Israel still adore,
Trust Him, praise Him evermore.

HYMN L.

HOW sad our State by Nature is,
  Our Sin how deep it stains!
And Satan binds our captive Souls
  Fast in his slavish Chains.

But there's a Voice of sov'reign Grace
  Sounds from GOD's sacred Word;
Ho! Ye despairing Sinners come,
  And trust upon the LORD.

O may we hear th' Almighty Call,
   And run to this Relief;
We wou'd believe thy Promise, LORD,
   O help our Unbelief!

To the blest Fountain of thy Blood,
   Teach us O LORD! to fly:
There may we wash our spotted Souls!
   From Crimes of deepest Dye!

Stretch out thine Arm, victorious King,
   Our reigning Sins subdue;
Drive the old Dragon from his Seat,
   And form our Souls anew.

Poor guilty, weak, and helpless Worms,
   On thy kind Arm we fall;
Be thou our Strength and Righteousness,
   Our JESUS and our All.

HYMN LI.

O Love divine, how sweet thou art!
   When shall we find each longing Heart
     All taken up by thee?
O! may we pant and thirst to prove,
The Greatness of redeeming Love,
     The Love of CHRIST so free.

GOD only knows the Love of GOD,
O that it now were shed abroad
     In each poor longing Heart!
For Love I'd sigh, for Love I'd pine,
This only Portion, LORD, be mine,
     Be mine this better Part.

O that we cou'd for ever sit,
With Mary, at the Master's Feet,
     Be this our happy Choice!

Our only Care, Delight, and Bliss,
Our Joy, our Heav'n on Earth be this,
    To hear the Bridegroom's Voice.

Thy only Love may we require,
Nothing on Earth beneath defire,
    Nothing in Heaven above:
Let Earth and all its Trifles go,
Give us, O Lord! thy Love to know,
    Give us thy precious Love.

HYMN LII.

MY Hiding-place, my Refuge, Tow'r,
    And Shield art thou, O Lord:
Give me to anchor all my Hopes
  On thy unerring Word.

Engrav'd as in eternal Brafs,
  The mighty Promife fhines,
Nor can the Pow'rs of Darknefs raze
  Thofe everlafting Lines.

The facred Word of Grace is ftrong,
  As that which built the Skies;
The Voice which rolls the Stars along,
  Spoke all the Promifes.

My Hiding-place, my Refuge, Tow'r,
  And Shield art thou, O Lord:
Give me to anchor all my Hopes
  On thy unerring Word.

HYMN LIII.

JESUS, thou art my Righteoufnefs,
    For all my Sins were thine;
Thy Death hath bought of God my Peace,
  Thy Life hath made Him mine;

My dying Saviour, and my GOD!
   Fountain for Guilt and Sin;
Sprinkle me ever with thy Blood,
   And cleanse, and keep me clean.

Wash me, and make me thus thine own;
   Wash me, and mine thou art;
Wash me, but not my Feet alone,
   My Hands, my Head, and Heart!
Th' Atonement of thy Blood apply,
   'Till Faith to Sight improve;
'Till Hope in full Enjoyment die,
   And all my Soul be Love!

HYMN LIV.

Hymns of Praise.

COME, let us join our chearful Songs
   With Angels round the Throne,
Ten thousand thousands are their Tongues,
   But all their Joys are one.

Worthy the Lamb that dy'd, they cry,
   To be exalted thus:
Worthy the Lamb, our Lips reply,
   For he was slain for us.

JESUS is worthy to receive
   Honour and Pow'r divine;
And Blessings more than we can give,
   Be, LORD, for ever thine.

The whole Creation join in one,
   To bless the sacred Name
Of Him that sits upon the Throne,
   And to adore the Lamb.

HYMN LV.

COME, happy Souls approach your GOD
  With new melodious Songs;
Come, tender to Almighty Grace
  The Tribute of your Tongues.

So strange, so boundless was the Love
  That pity'd dying Men,
The Father sent his equal Son,
  To give them Life again.

Thy Hands, dear JESUS, were not arm'd
  With a revenging Rod;
No hard Commission to perform
  The Vengeance of a GOD.

But all was Mercy, all was mild,
  And Wrath forsook the Throne,
When CHRIST on the kind Errand came,
  And brought Salvation down.

Here, Sinners, you may heal your Wounds,
  And wipe your Sorrows dry;
Trust in the mighty Saviour's Name,
  And you shall never die.

O dearest LORD, melt down our Souls
  T' accept thine offer'd Grace;
Then will we bless the Saviour's Love,
  And give the Father Praise.

HYMN LVI.

OH the Delights, the heav'nly Joys,
  The Glories of the Place,
Where JESUS sheds the brightest Beams
  Of his o'erflowing Grace!

Sweet Majesty and awful Love,
 Sit smiling on his Brow,
And all the glorious Ranks above
 At humble Distance bow.

His Head, the dear majestic Head
 That cruel Thorns did wound,
See what immortal Glories shine,
 And circle it around!

This is the Man, th' exalted Man,
 Whom we, unseen, adore;
But when our Eyes behold his Face,
 Our Hearts shall love him more.

Lord, set our Spirits all on fire
 To see thy bless'd Abode;
And tune our Tongues to sing the Praise
 Of our incarnate God!

HYMN LVII.

BEGIN, my Tongue, some heav'nly Theme,
 And speak some boundless Thing,
The mighty Works, or mightier Name,
 Our eternal King.

Tell of his wond'rous Faithfulness,
 And sound his Pow'r abroad,
Sing the sweet Promise of his Grace,
 And the performing God.

Proclaim Salvation from the Lord,
 For wretched dying Men;
His Hand hath writ the sacred Word
 With an immortal Pen.

Engrav'd as in eternal Brass
  The mighty Promise shines;
Nor can the Pow'rs of Darkness raze
  Those everlasting Lines.

O might we hear thine heav'nly Tongue
  But whisper, Thou art mine!
Those gentle Words should raise our Song
  To Notes almost divine.

How would our leaping Hearts rejoice,
  And think our Heav'n secure!
Give us to hear thy gracious Voice,
  And Faith desires no more.

HYMN LVIII.

O Thou, in whom the Gentiles trust,
  Thou only Holy, only Just,
Oh tune our Souls to praise thy Name,
Jesus! Uncheangeable, the Same!

If Angels, whilst to thee they sing,
Wrap up their Faces in their Wing,
How shall we, sinful Dust, draw nigh
The Great, the aweful Deity?

Glory to Thee, auspicious Lamb!
Thou holy Lord, thou great I AM:
With all our Pow'rs thy Grace we bless,
Our Joy, our Peace, our Righteousness.

Live, ever-glorious Jesus! live,
Worthy all Blessings to receive!
Worthy on high enthron'd to sit,
With ev'ry Pow'r beneath thy Feet.

HYMN LIX.

THOU dear Redeemer, dying Lamb,
   We love to hear of Thee;
No Mufic like thy charming Name
   Doth found fo fweet to me.
O may we ever hear thy Voice
   In Mercy to us fpeak,
And in our Prieft will we rejoice,
   Thou great Melchifedec.

Our JESUS fhall be ftill our Theme,
   While in this World we ftay,
We'll fing our JESU's lovely Name,
   When all Things elfe decay:
When we appear in yonder Cloud,
   With all his favour'd Throng,
Then will we fing more fweet, more loud,
   And CHRIST fhall be our Song

HYMN LX.

O Tell me no more
   Of this Worlds vain ftore,
The time for fuch Trifles
   Thro' Mercy is o'er.

A Canaan I've found
   Where true Joys abound,
'Tis heavenly dwelling
   On this happy Ground,

My Soul don't delay,
   He calls thee away,
Rife, follow thy Saviour;
   And blefs the glad Day.

The Souls that believe
  In Paradife live;
And me in that Number
  My Jesus receive!

No Mortal doth know
  What He can beftow,
What Light, Strength, and Comfort;
  Go after Him, go.

And when I'm to die,
  " Receive me," I'll cry;
For Jesus hath lov'd me,
  I cannot fay why!

And now I'm in Care,
  My Neighbours may fhare
Thefe Bleffings: To feek them
  Will none of you dare?

In Bondage, O why!
  And Death will you lie,
When One here affures you
  Free Grace is fo nigh!

HYMN LXI.

COME, let us all unite to blefs
    Jesus Christ, our Joy and Peace:
Let our Praife to Him be giv'n,
High at God's right Hand in Heav'n.

Mafter, fee, to Thee we bow,
Thou art Lord, and only Thou;
Thou, the bleffed Virgin's Seed,
Glory of thy Church, and Head.

Thee the Angels ceaseless sing;
Thee we praise, our Priest and King:
Worthy is thy Name of Praise,
Full of Glory, full of Grace!

Thou hast the glad Tidings brought
Of Salvation by Thee wrought;
Wrought—for all thy Church; and we
Worship in their Company.

We, thy little Flock, adore,
Thee, the LORD, for evermore:
Ever with us shew thy Love,
Till we join with those above.

HYMN LXII.

COME, let us ascend,
   My Companion and Friend,
To taste of a Banquet above;
  If thro' Mercy divine,
  For our JESUS we pine,
Let us mount the bless'd Chariot of Love.

  Who in JESUS confide,
  They are bold to outride
The Storms of Affliction beneath:
  With the Prophet they soar
  To that heav'nly Shore,
And outfly all the Arrows of Death.

  By Faith we are come
  To our permanent Home,
By Hope we the Rapture improve;
  By Love we still rise,
  And look down on the Skies—
For the Heaven of Heavens is Love!

Who on Earth can conceive
How happy we live
In the City of GOD the great King!
What a Concert of Praise,
When our JESUS's Grace,
The whole heav'nly Company sing!

What a rapturous Song,
When the glorify'd Throng
In the Spirit of Harmony join!
Join all the glad Choirs,
Hearts, Voices, and Lyres,
And the Burden is Mercy divine!

Hallelujah they cry
To the King of the Sky;
To the great everlasting I AM;
To the LAMB that was slain,
And liveth again:
Hallelujah to GOD and the LAMB!

HYMN LXIII.

HEAD of the Church triumphant!
We joyfully adore Thee,
Till thou appear,
Thy Members here
Shall sing like those in Glory.
We lift our Hearts and Voices
With blest Anticipation,
And cry aloud,
And give to GOD
The Praise of our Salvation.

While in Affliction's Furnace,
And paſſing thro' the Fire,
   Thy Love we praiſe,
   Which knows our Days,
And ever brings us nigher.
We clap our Hands exulting
In thine Almighty Favour,
   The Love divine
   Which made us thine
Shall keep us thine for ever.

Thou doſt conduct thy People
Thro' Torrents of Temptation,
   Nor will we fear,
   Whilſt thou art near,
The Fire of Tribulation.
The World, with Sin and Satan,
In vain our March oppoſes;
   By thee we ſhall
   Break thro' them all,
And ſing the Song of Moſes.

By Faith we ſee the Glory
To which thou ſhalt reſtore us,
   The Croſs deſpiſe
   For that high Prize
Which thou haſt ſet before us.
And if thou count us worthy,
We each, as dying Stephen,
   Shall ſee thee ſtand
   At God's right Hand,
To take us up to Heaven.

HYMN LXIV.

NOW to the LORD, a noble Song;
  Awake, my Soul, awake my Tongue,
Hosanna to th' eternal Name,
And all his boundless Love proclaim!

See where it shines in JESU's Face!
The brightest Image of his Grace;
GOD, in the Person of his Son,
Hath all his mightiest Works outdone.

Grace, 'tis a sweet, a charming Theme;
Exult, my Soul, at JESU's Name!
Ye Angels, dwell upon the Sound:
Ye Heav'ns, reflect it to the Ground!

Oh that we all may reach the Place,
Where He unveils his lovely Face;
Where all his Beauties you behold,
And sing his Name to Harps of Gold!

HYMN LXV.

TO GOD, the only wise,
  Our Saviour and our King,
Let all the Saints below the Skies,
  Their humble Praises bring.

'Tis his Almighty Love,
  His Counsel and his Care,
Preserves us safe from Sin and Death,
  And ev'ry hurtful Snare.

He will present his Saints,
  Unblemish'd and compleat,
Before the Glory of his Face,
  With Joys divinely great.

Then all the chosen Seed
Shall meet around the Throne,
Shall bless the Conduct of his Grace,
And make his Wonders known.

To our Redeemer-GOD,
Wisdom and Pow'r belongs,
Immortal Crowns of Majesty,
And everlasting Songs.

HYMN LXVI.

O What shall we do our Saviour to praise;
So faithful and true, so plenteous in Grace;
So strong to deliver, so good to redeem,
The weakest Believer, that hangs upon Him!

How happy the Man whose Heart is set free,
The People that can be joyful in Thee!
Their Joy is to walk in the Light of thy Face,
And still they are talking of JESUS's Grace.

Their daily Delight shall be in thy Name,
They shall, as their Right, thy Righteousness
(claim:
Thy Righteousness wearing, and cleans'd by thy
(Blood,
Bold shall they appear in the Presence of GOD.

HYMN LXVII.

WHAT shall we render unto Thee,
Thou glorious LORD of Life and Pow'r!
Teach us to bow the humble Knee,
Teach us with Thankfulness t' adore;
To praise Thee as thy Saints above,
To praise Thee for thy wond'rous Love.

When

When like loſt Sheep, we wander'd wide,
  And left the watchful Shepherd s Eye;
When borne along th' impetuous Tide,
  Of this World's Sin and Vanity;
    Our Jesus from the Heav'ns came down,
    To ſave us by his Grace alone.

He bore our Sins upon the Tree,
  (To ſeek and ſave the loſt He came)
There was He bound to ſet us free
  From Death and everlaſting Shame:
    The Captive Flock from Hell was freed,
    And ranſom'd when their Shepherd bled.

Before the Father's awful Throne,
  Our merciful High Prieſt yet ſtands,
And interceding for his own,
  The purchas'd Remnant now demands;
    His People's everlaſting Friend,
    Who loving—loves them to the End.

May we, his baniſh'd Ones, rejoice,
  Him for our Lord and God to own,
To take Him as our only Choice,
  And cleave to Him, in Love, alone:
    Still growing up in Holineſs,
    Till call'd to meet in Realms of Peace.

Then ſhall our grateful Songs abound,
  And ev'ry Tear be wip'd away;
No Sin, no Sorrow ſhall be found,
  No Night o'er-cloud the endleſs Day.
    O praiſe Him! all beneath, above,
    O praiſe Him! praiſe the God of Love!

HYMN LXVIII.

JESU, thy Blood and Righteousness,
  My Beauty are, my glorious Dress,
Midst flaming Worlds in these array'd,
With Joy shall I lift up my Head.

When from the Dust of Death I rise
To claim my Mansion in the Skies,
Ev'n then, shall this be all my Plea:
" JESUS hath *liv'd* and *dy'd* for me."

Bold shall I stand in that great Day,
For who ought to my Charge shall lay?
Fully thro' Thee absolv'd I am,
From Sin and Fear, from Guilt and Shame.

Thus Abraham, the Friend of GOD,
Thus all the Armies bought with Blood,
SAVIOUR of Sinners Thee proclaim,
Sinners, of whom the Chief I am.

This spotless Robe the same appears
When ruin'd Nature sinks in Years!
No Age can change its glorious Hue,
The Grace of CHRIST is ever new.

O! let the Dead now hear thy Voice,
Now bid thy banish'd Ones rejoice,
Their Beauty this, their glorious Dress,
JESUS, the LORD OUR RIGHTEOUSNESS.

HYMN LXIX.

RISE, my Soul, and stretch thy Wings,
  Thy better Portion trace;
Rise from transitory Things,
  Tow'rds Heav'n, thy native Place.

Sun, and Moon, and Stars decay,
  Time shall soon this Earth remove:
Rise, my Soul, and haste away
  To Seats prepar'd Above.

Rivers to the Ocean run,
  Nor stay in all their Course:
Fire ascending seeks the Sun,
  Both speed them to their Source:
So a Soul that's born of GOD
  Pants to view his glorious Face,
Upward tends to his Abode,
  To rest in his Embrace.

Cease, ye Pilgrims, cease to mourn;
  Press onward to the Prize;
Soon our Saviour will return
  Triumphant in the Skies:
Yet a Season, and you know
  Happy Entrance will be giv'n,
All our Sorrows left below,
  And Earth exchang'd for Heav'n.

HYMN LXX.

WHO can have greater Cause to sing,
  Who greater Cause to bless,
Than we, the Children of the King,
  Than we, who CHRIST possess? &c.

With Angel-Hosts, dear Lamb, we join
  To praise thy Love and Pow'r,
To magnify thy Grace divine,
  Thou mighty Counsellor.

We late were Satan's Captives led,
  And Hell had been our End,
Hadst Thou not for our Pardon bled,
  Thou Sinners only Friend.

For this we ne'er wou'd hold our Tongue,
  Nor let our Praises cease;
We evermore wou'd sing that Song,
  THE LORD OUR RIGHTEOUSNESS.

No other GOD we'd know but Thee,
  None else did us create:
Thy Glory may we ever be,
  O holy Advocate.

'Twas Thou, 'twas only Thou didst take
  The Mediator's Place.
When we the Father's Statutes brake,
  All hail! thou Prince of Peace.

O may we prove Thee still the same,
  Whene'er our Need we see;
Thou bearest still a Saviour's Name,
  Our Saviour thou shalt be!

No Law, nor Sin, nor Hell, nor Death,
  Can us from Thee divide;
Give us to hold this precious Faith,
  FOR US OUR SAVIOUR DY'D.

HYMN LXXI.

REJOICE, the LORD is King!
  Your Lord and King adore,
Mortals give Thanks and sing,
  And triumph evermore:
Lift up your Heart, lift up your Voice,
Rejoice, again I say, rejoice.

JESUS the Saviour reigns,
  The GOD of Truth and Love,
When He had purg'd our Stains,
  He took his Seat above:
Lift up your Heart, lift up your Voice,
Rejoice, again I say, rejoice.

His Kingdom cannot fail,
  He rules o'er Earth and Heav'n,
The Keys of Death and Hell
  Are to our JESUS giv'n:
Lift up your Heart, lift up your Voice,
Rejoice, again I say, rejoice.

He sits at GOD's right Hand
  Till all his Foes submit,
And bow to his Command,
  And fall beneath his Feet:
Lift up your Heart, lift up your Voice,
Rejoice, again I say, rejoice.

Rejoice in glorious Hope,
  JESUS the Judge shall come,
And take his Servants up
  To their eternal Home:
We soon shall hear th' Archangel's Voice,
The Trump of GOD shall sound, Rejoice.

HYMN LXXII.

AWAKE, and sing the Song
  Of Moses and the Lamb,
Wake ev'ry Heart and ev'ry Tongue
  To praise the Saviour's Name.

Sing of his dying Love,
  Sing of his rising Pow'r,
Sing how He interceeds above
  For those whose Sins he bore.

Sing 'till we feel our Hearts
  Ascending with our Tongues,
Sing till the Love of Sin departs,
  And Grace inspires our Songs.

 Sing on your heav'nly Way,
  Ye ransom'd Sinners sing,
Sing on, rejoicing ev'ry Day
  In CHRIST th' eternal King.

 Soon shall ye hear Him say,
  " Ye blessed Children come;"
Soon will He call ye hence away,
  And take his Wand'rers Home.

HYMN LXXIII.

JOIN all the glorious Names
  Of Wisdom, Love, and Power,
 That Mortals never knew,
  That Angels ever bore:
All are too mean to speak his Worth,
Too mean to set our Saviour forth.

 But, O what gentle Terms,
  What condescending Ways,
 Doth our Redeemer use
  To teach his heav'nly Grace!
My Soul, with Joy and Wonder see
What Forms of Love CHRIST bears for Thee.

 Great Prophet of our GOD,
  Our Tongues would bless thy Name!
 By Thee the joyful News
  Of our Salvation came;
The joyful News of Sins forgiv'n,
Of Hell subdu'd, and Peace with Heav'n.

 JESUS, our great High Priest,
  Offer'd his Blood and dy'd;
 Thou guilty Sinner seek
  No Sacrifice beside:
His pow'rful Blood did once atone,
And now it pleads before the Throne.

Thou dear Almighty LORD,
Our Conqu'ror and our King,
Thy Scepter and thy Sword,
Thy reigning Grace we sing.
Thine is the Pow'r: O may we sit,
In willing Bonds, beneath thy Feet!

HYMN LXXIV.

ARRAY'd in mortal Flesh,
CHRIST like an Angel stands,
And holds the Promises
And Pardons in his Hands:
Commission'd from his Father's Throne,
To make his Grace to Mortals known.

Be Thou our Counsellor,
Our Pattern and our Guide!
And through this desert Land
Still keep us near thy Side!
O let our Feet ne'er run astray,
Nor rove, nor seek the crooked Way!

Sweet is the Shepherd's Voice,
Who's watchful Eye doth keep
Poor wand'ring Souls among
The Thousands of his Sheep,
He feeds his Flock, He calls their Names,
His Bosom bears the tender Lambs.

To this dear Surety's Hands,
My Soul, commend thy Cause,
He answers and fulfils
His Father's broken Laws:
Believing Souls now free are set:
For CHRIST hath paid their dreadful Debt.

Their Advocate appears
For their Defence on high,
The Father bows his Ears,
And lays his Thunder by;
Not all that Hell or Sin can say,
Shall turn his Heart, his Love away.

Then let our Souls arise,
And tread the Tempter down;
Our Captain leads us forth
To Conquest and a Crown.
A feeble Saint shall win the Day,
Tho' Death and Hell obstruct the Way.

HYMN LXXV.

COME thou Source of ev'ry Blessing!
    Tune our Hearts to sing thy Grace!
Streams of Mercy never-ceasing,
    Call for Songs of loudest Praise:
Teach us some melodious Sonnet,
    Sung by flaming Tongues above;
Praise the Mount;—O fix us on it,
    Mount of GOD's unchanging Love!

Here we raise our Eben-Ezer,
    Hither by thine Help we're come;
And we trust by thy good Pleasure,
    Safely to arrive at Home:
JESUS sought us all when Strangers,
    Wand'ring from the Fold of GOD,
He, to rescue us from Dangers,
    Interpos'd his precious Blood.

O! to Grace, what mighty Debtors
    Daily we're constrain'd to be!
Let that Grace, like strongest Fetters,
    Bind our wand'ring Hearts to Thee!

Prone to wander, LORD, we feel them,
  Prone to leave the GOD of Love —
Take our Hearts—O take, and seal them!
  Seal them from thy Courts above!

HYMN LXXVI.

THE LORD supplies his People's Need,
  JEHOVAH is his Name:
In Pastures fresh he makes them feed
  Beside the living Stream.

He brings their wand'ring Spirits back,
  When they forsake his Ways,
And leads them, for his Mercy's Sake,
  In Paths of Truth and Grace.

When they walk thro' the Shades of Death,
  His Presence is their Stay:
A Word of his supporting Breath,
  Drives all their Fears away.

His Hand in Sight of all their Foes
  Doth still their Table spread,
Their Cup with Blessings overflows,
  His Oil anoints their Head.

The sure Provisions of our GOD
  Attend us all our Days:
O may his House be our Abode,
  And all our Work his Praise.

HYMN LXXVII.

BURY'D in Shadows of the Night,
  We lie till CHRIST restores the Light;
Wisdom descends to heal the Blind,
And chace the Darkness of the Mind.

Lost guilty Souls are drown'd in Tears,
Till the atoning Blood appears;
Then they awake from deep Distress,
And sing the LORD OUR RIGHTEOUSNESS.

JESUS beholds where Satan reigns,
Binding his Slaves in heavy Chains:
He sets the Pris'ner free, and breaks
The iron Bondage from our Necks.

Poor helpless Worms in Thee possess
Grace, Wisdom, Power, and Righteousness;
Thou art our mighty All, may we
Give our whole Selves, O LORD, to Thee!

HYMN LXXVIII.

OUR Shepherd alone,
   The LORD, let us bless,
Who reigns on the Throne,
   The Prince of our Peace;
Who evermore saves us
   By shedding his Blood;
All hail, holy JESUS,
   Our LORD and our GOD!

We daily will sing
   Thy Merits, thy Praise,
Thou merciful Spring
   Of Pity and Grace:
Thy Kindness for ever
   To Men we will tell;
And say, Our dear Saviour
   Redeems us from Hell.

Preserve us in Love,
   While here we abide;
Nor ever remove
   Nor cover, nor hide
Thy glorious Salvation,
   Till joyful we see
The beautiful Vision
   Completed in Thee!

HYMN LXXIX. Psalm C.

BEFORE Jehovah's awful Throne,
   Ye Nations bow with sacred Joy,
Know that the Lord is God alone!
He can create, and He destroy.

His sov'reign Pow'r without our Aid,
Made us of Clay, and form'd us Men:
And when like wand'ring Sheep we stray'd,
He brought us to his Fold again.

We'll croud thy Gates with thankful Songs,
High as the Heav'ns our Voices raise;
And Earth with her ten thousand Tongues
Shall fill thy Courts with sounding Praise.

Wide as the World is thy Command,
Vast as Eternity thy Love,
Firm as a Rock thy Truth must stand,
When rolling Years shall cease to move.

HYMN LXXX.

LOVE divine, all Love excelling,
   Joy of Heaven, to Earth come down!
Fix us in thy humble Dwelling,
All thy faithful Mercies crown:

Jesus! Thou art all Compaſſion,
Pure unbounded Love Thou art,
Viſit us with thy Salvation,
Enter ev'ry trembling Heart!

Breathe! O breathe thy loving Spirit
Into ev'ry troubled Breaſt!
Let us all in Thee inherit,
Let us find thy promis'd Reſt:
Take away the Love of ſinning,
Alpha and Omega be,
End of Faith, as its Beginning,
Set our Hearts at Liberty.

Come! Almighty to deliver,
Let us Life and Pow'r receive!
Come, poſſeſs our Hearts, and never,
Never, Lord, thy Temples leave!
Thee we would be always bleſſing,
Serve Thee as thine Hoſts Above,
Bleſs, and praiſe Thee without ceaſing,
Glory in thy changeleſs Love.

Carry on thy new Creation,
Happy, holy, may we be,
Let us ſee thy great Salvation,
Join'd in Spirit unto Thee!
Chang'd from Glory into Glory,
Till in Heaven we take our Place,
Till we caſt our Crowns before Thee,
Loſt in Wonder, Love, and Praiſe.

HYMN LXXXI.

YE Servants of God,
   Your Maſter proclaim,
And publiſh abroad
   His wonderful Name,

The Name all victorious
 Of JESUS extol;
His Kingdom is glorious,
 And rules over all.

GOD ruleth on high,
 Almighty to save,
And still He is nigh,
 His Presence we have.
The great Congregation,
 His Triumph shall sing,
Ascribing Salvation
 To JESUS our King.

Salvation to GOD,
 Who sits on the Throne;
Let all cry aloud,
 And honour the Son,
Our JESUS's Praises
 The Angels proclaim,
Fall down on their Faces,
 And worship the Lamb.

Then let us adore,
 And give Him his Right,
All Glory and Pow'r,
 And Wisdom, and Might;
All Honour and Blessing,
 With Angels Above,
And Thanks never ceasing,
 And infinite Love.

HYMN LXXXII.

HOW can we adore,
 Or worthily praise
Thy Goodness and Pow'r,
 Thou GOD of all Grace!

With Honour and Blessing,
 Before Thee we fall,
Most gladly confessing
 Thee Father of all.

The Heav'ns and Earth,
 And Water, and Air,
To Thee owe their Birth,
 Subsist by thy Care;
While Angels are singing
 Thy Praises above,
We mortals are bringing
 Our Tribute of Love.

Thou, Saviour, art One
 With God the Supreme,
His eternal Son,
 And equal with Him:
Invested with Glory,
 On high dost Thou sit,
While Angels adore Thee,
 And bow at thy Feet.

How great was thy Love!
 How wond'rous thy Grace!
Thou cam'st from above
 To save a lost Race;
And, Man to deliver,
 Of Mary wast born,
That ev'ry Believer
 To God might return.

How soon will thy Seat
 Of Judgment appear!
Prepare us to meet
 And welcome Thee there.

Thy witnessing Spirit
  In us shed abroad,
And bid us inherit
  The Kingdom of God.

The Father and Son
  And Spirit agree,
To constitute one
  Compleat Deity:
Immanuel's Merit
  Makes our Peace with God,
And by the good Spirit
  Our Souls are renew'd.

HYMN LXXXIII.

BLESSED are the Sons of God,
They are bought with Christ's own Blood,
They are ransom'd from the Grave,
Life eternal they shall have.

God did love them in his Son,
Long before the World begun;
They the Seal of this receive
When on Jesus they believe.

They are justify'd by Grace,
They enjoy a solid Peace;
All their Sins are wash'd away,
They shall stand in God's great Day.

They produce the Fruits of Grace,
In the Works of Righteousness!
They are harmless, meek and mild,
Holy, humble, undefil'd.

They are Lights upon the Earth,
Children of an heav'nly Birth;
Born of God; they hate all Sin,
God's pure Seed remains within.

They have Fellowſhip with GOD,
Thro' the Mediator's Blood;
One with GOD, with JESUS one,
Glory is in them begun.

Tho' they ſuffer much on Earth,
Strangers quite to this World's Mirth,
Yet they have an inward Joy,
Pleaſure which can never cloy.

They alone are truly bleſt,
Heirs of GOD, joint Heirs with CHRIST;
With them number'd may we be,
Here and in Eternity!

HYMN LXXXIV.

COME, ye that love the LORD,
   And let your Joys be known,
Join in a Song with ſweet Accord,
   While ye ſurround the Throne.

The Sorrows of the Mind
   Be baniſh'd from this Place;
Religion never was deſign'd
   To make our Comforts leſs.

Let thoſe refuſe to ſing
   Who never knew our GOD;
But Children of the heav'nly King
   Will ſpeak their Joys abroad.

The Men of Grace have found
   Glory begun below;
Celeſtial Fruits on earthly Ground,
   From Faith and Hope ſhall grow.

The Hill of Zion yields
  A thousand sacred Sweets,
Before we reach the heav'nly Fields,
  Or walk the golden Streets.

Then let our Songs abound,
  And ev'ry Tear be dry,
We're marching thro' Immanuel's Ground
  To fairer Worlds on high.

HYMN LXXXV.

CHILDREN of the heav'nly King,
  As ye journey sweetly sing:
Sing your Saviour's worthy Praise,
Glorious in his Works and Ways!

Ye are trav'ling home to God,
In the Way the Fathers trod;
They are happy now, and ye
Soon their Happiness shall see.

O, ye banish'd Seed, be glad!
Christ our Advocate is made;
Us to save our Flesh assumes,
Brother to our Souls becomes.

Shout, ye little Flock, and blest,
You on Jesu's Throne shall rest;
There your Seat is now prepar'd,
There your Kingdom and Reward.

Fear not, Brethren, joyful stand
On the Borders of your Land;
Jesus Christ, your Father's Son,
Bids you undismay'd go on.

Lord! obediently we'll go,
Gladly leaving all below;
Only Thou our Leader be,
And we still will follow Thee!

HYMN LXXXVI.

THE Lord crucify'd,
    The Saviour that dy'd,
Hath call'd, and betroth'd us, and made us his
                                  [Bride,
    He freely came down
    To give a rich Crown,
To those who had nothing but Sin of their own.

    O what a vast Depth,
    Discover'd by Faith,
Of infinite Mercy in JESUS's Death!

    'Tis there that we see
    Salvation is free,
And hear, *It is finish'd*, on Calvary's Tree.

    Then here would we lay,
    Submissive as Clay,
Till th' Archangel's Trumpet proclaims the last
                                  [Day.
    Then joyful awake,
    Corruption forsake,
And JESUS's Image in Glory partake.

HYMN LXXXVII. A Dialogue.

TELL us, O Women, we would know,
    Whither so fast ye move?
We, call'd to leave the World below,
    Are seeking one above.

Whence come ye, say, and what the Place
    That ye are trav'ling from?
From Tribulation, we, through Grace,
    Are now returning home.

Is not your native Country here?
 Like you not this Abode?
We seek a better Country far,
 A City built by G O D.

Thither we travel, nor intend
 Short of that Bliss to rest;
Nor we, till in the Sinner's Friend
 Our weary Souls are bless'd.

Friends of the Bridegroom we shall reign;
 Saviour, we ask no more;
Hail, Lamb of G O D! for Sinners slain,
 Whom Heaven and Earth adore.

HYMN LXXXVIII.

YE Souls that are weak,
 And helpless, and poor,
Who know not to speak,
 Much less to do more:
Lo! here's a Foundation
 For Comfort and Peace;
In CHRIST is Salvation,
 The Kingdom is his.

With Power he rules,
 And Wonders performs;
Gives Conduct to Fools,
 And Courage to Worms,
Beset by sore Evils
 Without and within,
By Legions of Devils,
 And Mountains of Sin.

Then be not afraid,
  All Power is given
To JESUS our Head,
  In Earth and in Heav'n;
Thro' Him we shall conquer
  The mightiest Foes;
Our Captain is stronger
  Than all that oppose.

His Pow'r from above
  He'll kindly impart;
So free is his Love,
  So tender his Heart!
Redeem'd with his Merit,
  We're wash'd in his Blood;
Renew'd by his Spirit,
  We've Power with GOD.

Thy Grace we adore,
  Director divine;
The Kingdom, and Pow'r,
  And Glory, are thine:
Preserve us from running
  On Rocks, or on Shelves,
From Foes strong and cunning,
  But most from Ourselves.

Reign o'er us as King;
  Accomplish thy Will;
And each of us bring
  To Zion's bless'd Hill;
There falling before Thee,
  We'll praise thy lov'd Name,
And ever adore Thee
  For ever the same.

HYMN LXXXIX.

WHAT equal Honours shall we bring,
 To Thee, O Lord our God, the Lamb?
Since all the Notes that Angels sing,
Are far inferior to thy Name.

Worthy is He that once was slain,
The Prince of Peace that gron'd and dy'd;
Worthy to rise, and live, and reign
At his Almighty Father's Side.

Pow'r and Dominion are his Due
Who stood condemn'd at Pilate's Bar;
Wisdom belongs to Jesus too,
Tho' he was charg'd with Madness here.

Honour immortal must be paid,
Instead of Scandal and of Scorn;
While Glory shines around his Head,
And a bright Crown without a Thorn.

Blessings for ever on the Lamb,
Who bore our Sins, and Curse, and Pain;
Let Angels sound his sacred Name,
And ev'ry Creature say, Amen.

HYMN XC.

GLORY be to God on high,
 God whose Glory fills the Sky;
Peace on Earth to Man forgiv'n,
Man the well-belov'd of Heav'n.

Sov'reign Father, heav'nly King,
Thee we now presume to sing;
Glad thine Attributes confess,
Glorious all and numberless.

Hail! by all thy Works ador'd,
Hail! the everlasting LORD:
Thee with thankful Hearts we prove,
LORD of Pow'r, and GOD of Love.

CHRIST our LORD and GOD we own,
CHRIST the Father's only Son;
Lamb of GOD for Sinners slain,
Saviour of offending Man!

Pow'rful Advocate with GOD,
Justify us by thy Blood;
Bow thine Ear, in Mercy bow,
Hear the World's Atonement Thou!

Hear; for Thou, O CHRIST, alone,
Co-equal with the LORD, art One!
One the Holy Ghost, with Thee,
One Supreme eternal Three.

HYMN XCI.

HOW glorious the Lamb
  Is seen on his Throne!
His Labours are o'er,
  His Conquests put on:
A Kingdom is giv'n
  Into the Lamb's Hand,
In Earth and in Heav'n,
  For ever to stand.

Ye Sinners below
  Then trust in the LORD,
Look up to his Arm,
  His Honour, his Word:
Athirst for his Favour,
  His Godhead adore;
Look up to your Saviour,
  And joy evermore!

HYMN XCII.

GIVE Thanks to God most high,
The universal Lord,
The sov'reign King of Kings,
And be his Grace ador'd.
 His Pow'r and Grace
 Are still the same,
 And let his Name
 Have endless Praise.

How mighty is his Hand!
What Wonders hath He done!
He form'd the Earth and Seas,
And spread the Heav'ns alone.
 Thy Mercy, Lord,
 Shall still endure,
 And ever sure
 Abides thy Word.

He saw the Nations lie,
All perishing in Sin,
And pity'd the sad State,
The ruin'd World was in.
 Thy Mercy, Lord,
 Shall still endure,
 And ever sure
 Abides thy Word.

He sent his only Son
To save us from our Woe,
From Satan, Sin, and Death,
And ev'ry hurtful Foe.
 His Pow'r and Grace
 Are still the same,
 And let his Name
 Have endless Praise.

HYMN XCIII.

AWAKE, our Souls, away our Fears;
Let ev'ry trembling Thought be gone;
Awake and run the heav'nly Race:
And put a chearful Courage on.

True 'tis a ſtrait and thorny Road,
And mortal Spirits tire and faint:
But we forget the mighty GOD,
That feeds the Strength of every Saint.

O mighty GOD, thy matchleſs Pow'r!
Is ever new and ever young;
And firm endures, while endleſs Years
Their everlaſting Circles run.

From Thee, the overflowing Spring,
Believers drink a freſh Supply,
While ſuch as truſt their native Strength,
Shall melt away, and droop, and die.

Swift as an Eagle cuts the Air,
O may we mount to thine Abode!
On Wings of Love to JESUS fly,
Nor tire amidſt the heav'nly Road!

HYMN XCIV.

ZION's a Garden wall'd around,
Choſen and made peculiar Ground;
A little Spot incloſ'd by Grace,
Out of the World's wide Wilderneſs.

Like Spicy Trees, Believers ſtand,
Planted by an Almighty Hand;
And all the Springs in Zion flow,
To make the rich Plantation grow.

Awake, O heav'nly Wind, and come,
Blow on this Garden of Perfume;
Spirit divine, descend, and breathe
A gracious Gale on Plants beneath.

Make Thou our Spices flow abroad,
A grateful Incense to our God;
Let Faith, and Love, and Joy appear,
And ev'ry Grace be active here.

HYMN XCV.

THY Favours Lord, surprize our Souls,
   Will the Eternal dwell with us?
What canst thou find beneath the Poles,
To tempt thy Chariot downward thus?

Still might he fill his starry Throne,
And please his Ears with Gabriel's Songs;
But th' heav'nly Majesty comes down,
And bows to hearken to our Tongues.

Great God! what poor Returns we pay,
For Love so infinite as thine?
Words are but Air, and Tongues but Clay:
But all thy Mercies are divine.

HYMN XCVI.

THE Fountain of Christ
   Assist us to sing,
The Blood of our Priest,
   Our crucify'd King:
Which perfectly cleanses
   From Sin and from Filth,
And richly dispenses
   Salvation and Health.

The Fountain so dear
  He'll freely impart,
When pierc'd by the Spear,
  It flow'd from his Heart;
With Blood and with Water,
  The first to atone,
To cleanse us the latter;
  The Fountain's but one.

This Fountain from Guilt
  Not only makes pure,
And gives, soon as felt,
  Infallible Cure:
But if Guilt removed
  Return, and remain,
Its Pow'r may be proved
  Again, and again.

This Fountain unseal'd
  Stands open for all,
That long to be heal'd,
  The Great and the Small;
Here's Strength for the weakly
  That hither are led;
Here's Health for the sickly;
  Here's Life for the Dead.

This Fountain, tho' rich,
  From Charge is quite clear;
The poorer the Wretch
  The welcomer here,
Come needy, come guilty,
  Come lothesome, and bare;
You can't come too filthy—
  Come just as you are.

This Fountain in vain
  Has never been try'd,
It takes out all Stain
  Whenever apply'd:
The Water flows sweetly
  With Virtue divine,
To cleanse Souls completely,
  Tho' leprous as mine.

HYMN XCVII.

O COME let us join,
  Together combine,
To praise our dear Saviour our Master divine.

Him let us adore,
Who cover'd with Gore,
Late hanged on Calv'ry, both wounded and poor.

He worthy is bless'd,
By Spirits at rest,
Who once in this Desert his Godhead confess'd.

The heav'nly Spheres,
Who saw Him in Tears,
Yea ev'ry blest Angel, his Person reveres.

The Prophets who told
His Suff'rings of old,
Sing now sweet Thanksgiving on Psalteries of
  (Gold.

The Fathers to whom
He shew'd He would come,
Now in his Pavilion, take up their long Home.

The Spirits of Men,
Who for Him were flain,
From Abel the Righteous, fhare now in his
(Reign.

The Apoſtles who ſtood,
Refifting to Blood,
For Jesus's Gofpel, rejoice in their God.

The Confeffors too,
Them proſtrating low,
Caſt down their bright Mitres, and thankfully
(bow.

To Him that was flain,
The fcorn'd Nazarene,
Be Glory and Honour: let all fay, Amen.

HYMN XCVIII.

COME, and let us fweetly join,
Christ to praife in Hymns divine;
Give we all with one Accord,
Glory to our common Lord:
Strive we, in Affection ſtrive,
Let the purer Flame revive,
Such as in the Martyrs glow'd,
Dying Champions for their God.

Sing we then in Jesu's Name,
Now, as Yefterday the fame;
One in ev'ry Age and Place,
Full of Love, of Truth, and Grace:
Christ is now gone up on high,
(Thither may our Wifhes fly:)
Sits at God's right Hand above,
There with Him we reign in Love!

HYMN XCIX.

A Spur for Professors.

Lukewarm Souls, the Foe grows stronger,
  See what Hosts your Camp surround,
Arm to Battle; lag no longer.
  Hark! the Silver Trumpets sound.
Wake, ye Sleepers; wake. What mean you?
  Sin besets you round about.
Up, and search. The World's within you,
  Slay, or chase the Traitor out.

What enchants you; Pelf, or Pleasure?
  Pluck right Eyes; with right Hands part.
Ask your Conscience, Where's your Treasure?
  For, be certain, there's your Heart.
Give the fawning Foe no Credit.
  Lo! the bloody Flag's unfurl'd.
That base Heart (the Word has said it)
  Loves not God, that loves the World.

God and Mammon? Oh! be wiser.
  Serve them Both? It cannot be.
Ease in Warfare, Saint and Miser,
  These will ne'er at all agree.
Shun the Shame of foully falling
  Cumber'd Captives clogg'd with Clay.
Prove your Faith. Make sure your Calling.
  Wield the Sword; and win the Day.

Forward press toward Perfection.
  Watch, and pray; and all Things prove.
Seek to know your God's Election;
  Search his everlasting Love.

Dread Backsliding, scorn Dissembling,
  Now Salvation's near in View.
Work it out, with Fear and Trembling:
  'Tis your GOD that works in You.

HYMN C.

GUIDE us, O Thou great JEHOVAH,
  Pilgrims, thro' this barren Land,
We are weak, but Thou art mighty;
Hold us with thy pow'rful Hand:
Bread of Heav'n, Bread of Heav'n,
Feed us till we want no more.

Open now the crystal Fountain
Whence the healing Streams do flow,
Let the fiery cloudy Pillar
Lead us all our Journey thro':
Strong Deliv'rer, strong Deliv'rer,
Be Thou still our Strength and Shield.

When we tread the Verge of Jordan,
Bid our anxious Fears subside;
Death of Deaths, and Hell's Destruction,
Land us safe on Canaan's side:
Songs of Praises, Songs of Praises,
We will ever give to Thee.

HYMN CI.

On taking a Member into Society.

WELCOME, Thou well-belov'd of GOD,
  Thou Heir of Grace, redeem'd by Blood;
Welcome with us thine Hand to join,
As Partner of our Lot divine:
  Blessings abundant from above,
  Give *Him*, we pray, Thou GOD of Love.

With us the Pilgrims' State embrace;
We're trav'ling to a blissful Place,
The new Jerusalem above,
The radiant Throne, the Seat of Love.
   The Holy Ghost that knows the Way,
   Conduct thee on from Day to Day!

The Staff of Promise now receive,
Thy weary Footsteps to relieve,
The chief Support the Trav'ler knows,
Leaning on which he forward goes.
   Thus if for Rest thy Spirits call,
   Leaning on this thou can'st not fall.

With Peace, with ceaseless Peace be shod,
The Shoes of Peace receive of God;
These keep from Pain the Pilgrim's Feet,
And make the rugged Way seem sweet;
   So Sion's Paths shall ever prove
   The Paths of Joy, and Peace, and Love.

Thus onward move with upright Pace;
Stedfast pursue the Gospel-Race.
Fill'd with the Pow'r of Truth divine,
Prove all the Strength of JESUS thine.
   Commission'd Angels soon shall come,
   And waft thee to thy wish'd-for Home.

HYMN CII.

Upon going forth to Preach.

FORTH in thy Strength, O LORD, we go,
   Thy Gospel to proclaim,
Thine only Righteousness to shew,
   And glorify thy Name.

Vouchsafe thine Aid to speak thy Word
  In this appointed Hour!
Attend it with thy Spirit, LORD,
  And let it come with Pow'r.

Open the Hearts of all that hear,
  To make their Saviour Room,
Now let them find Redemption near,
  Let Faith by Hearing come.

Give them to hear the Word as thine,
  And while they thus receive,
Prove it the saving Pow'r divine,
  To Sinners that believe.

HYMN CIII.
After returning from Preaching.

GLORY to Thee our CHRIST be giv'n,
  For this thy Gospel Word,
Thanks for the News reveal'd from Heav'n,
  SALVATION from the LORD.

Glory to thy great Name alone,
  That Life and Pow'r imparts;
Now, LORD, thy Gospel-Message own,
  And graft it on their Hearts.

Now let them feel the Tidings true,
  Grant to thy Word Success;
Water it with thy heav'nly Dew,
  And give the wish'd Increase.

Savour of Life! O let it prove,
  And shew their Sins forgiv'n!
Give them that Faith which works by Love,
  Which sweetly leads to Heav'n.

FESTIVAL HYMNS.

HYMN CIV. Christ's Nativity.

HARK! the Herald-Angels sing,
   Glory to the new-born King!
Peace on Earth and Mercy mild,
God and Sinners reconcil'd.

Joyful all ye Nations rise;
Join the Triumphs of the Skies;
With th' angelic Host proclaim,
" Christ is born in Bethlehem!"

Christ, by highest Heaven ador'd;
Christ, the Everlasting Lord;
Late in Time behold Him come,
Offspring of a Virgin's Womb.

Veil'd in Flesh the Godhead see;
Hail th' incarnate Deity!
Pleas'd as Man with Men t' appear,
Jesus our Immanuel here.

Hail the Heav'n-born Prince of Peace!
Hail the Sun of Righteousness!
Light and Life to all He brings,
Ris'n with Healing in his Wings.

Mild he lays his Glory by,
Born, that Man no more may die;
Born to raise the Sons of Earth,
Born to give them second Birth.

Come, Desire of Nations, come,
Fix in us thy humble Home;
Rise the Woman's conqu'ring Seed,
Bruise in us the Serpent's Head.

Adam's Likeness now efface,
Stamp thine Image in its Place;
Second Adam from above,
Re-instate us in thy Love!

HYMN CV. *The same.*

COME, thou long-expected Jesus,
   Born to set thy People free;
From our Fears and Sins release us,
   Let us find our Rest in Thee!
Isr'el's Strength and Consolation,
   Hope of all the Earth Thou art;
Dear Desire of ev'ry Nation,
   Joy of ev'ry longing Heart!

Born thy People to deliver;
   Born a Child, and yet a King;
Born to reign in us for ever,
   Now thy gracious Kingdom bring!
By thine own eternal Spirit,
   Rule in all our Hearts alone;
By thine all-sufficient Merit,
   Raise us to thy glorious Throne!

HYMN CVI.

The Crucifixion of CHRIST.

HEARTS of Stone, relent, relent,
   Break, by Jesu's Cross subdu'd;
See his Body mangled, rent,
   Cover'd with a Gore of Blood!
Sinful Soul, what hast Thou done?
Murder'd GOD's eternal Son!

Yes, our Sins have done the Deed,
  Drove the Nails that fix Him there,
Crown'd with Thorns his sacred Head,
  Pierc'd Him with a Soldier's Spear,
Made his Soul a Sacrifice;
For a sinful World he dies.

Shall we let Him die in vain?
  Still to Death pursue our GOD?
Open tear his Wounds again,
  Trample on his precious Blood?
Teach us with our Sins to part,
JESUS give a broken Heart.

HYMN CVII. *The same.*

"'TIS finish'd," the Redeemer said,
  And meekly bow'd his dying Head.
    Whilst we this Sentence scan,
Come, Sinners, and observe the Word,
Behold the Conquests of our LORD,
    Compleat for helpless Men.

Finish'd the Righteousness of Grace,
Finish'd for Sinners pard'ning Peace;
    Their mighty Debt is paid:
Accusing Law cancell'd by Blood,
And Wrath of an offended GOD
    In sweet Oblivion laid.

Who now shall urge a second Claim?
The Law no longer can condemn,
    Faith a Release can shew:
Justice itself a Friend appears;
The Prison-House a Whisper hears,
    " Loose him and let him go."

O Unbelief! injurious Bar!
Source of tormenting fruitless Fear,
 Why doſt thou yet reply?
Where'er thy loud Objections fall,
" 'Tis finiſh'd," ſtill may anſwer all,
 And ſilence ev'ry Cry.

  N. B. *See Hymns for the* SACRAMENT.

HYMN CVIII.

The Reſurrection of CHRIST.

THE Sun of Righteouſneſs appears,
 To ſet in Blood no more;
Adore the Scatterer of your Fears,
 Your riſing GOD adore.

The Saints, when he reſign'd his Breath,
 Uncloſ'd their ſleeping Eyes;
He breaks again the Bands of Death,
 Again the Dead ariſe.

Alone the dreadful Race he ran,
 Alone the Wine-preſs trod:
He dy'd and ſuffer'd as a Man,
 He riſes as a GOD.

In vain the Stone, the Watch, the Seal,
 Forbid an early Riſe
To Him who breaks the Gates of Hell,
 And opens Paradiſe.

HYMN CIX. *The ſame.*

CHRIST the LORD is riſen to-day! *Hallelujah!*
 Sons of Men and Angels ſay, *Hallelujah!*
Raiſe your Joys and Triumphs high, *Hallelujah!*
Sing, ye Heav'ns, and Earth reply, *Hallelujah!*

Love's redeeming Work is done,
Fought the Fight, the Battle won:
Lo! our Sun's Eclipse is o'er,
Lo! He sets in Blood no more.

Vain the Stone, the Watch, the Seal,
CHRIST hath burst the Gates of Hell:
Death in vain forbids his Rise,
CHRIST hath open'd Paradise.

Lives again our glorious King,
Where, O Death, is now thy Sting!
Once he dy'd our Souls to save;
Where's thy Vict'ry, O Grave!

Soar we now where CHRIST has led,
Foll'wing our exalted Head:
Made like Him, like Him we rise,
Ours the Cross, the Grave, the Skies.

What tho' once we perish'd all,
Partners of our Parent's Fall;
Second Life we now receive,
In our heav'nly Adam live.

Hail the LORD of Earth and Heav'n!
Praise to Thee by Both be giv'n!
Thee we greet triumphant now,
Hail! the RESURRECTION—THOU!

King of Glory! Soul of Bliss!
Everlasting Life is this—
Thee to know—Thy Pow'r to prove,
Thus to sing, and thus to love.

  N. B. *See Hymns for the* LORD's-DAY.

HYMN CX.

The Ascension of Christ.

OUR Lord is risen from the Dead,
  Our Jesus is gone up on high,
The Pow'rs of Hell are captive led,
Dragg'd to the Portals of the Sky.

There his triumphal Chariot waits,
And Angels chant the solemn Lay,
Lift up your Heads, ye heav'nly Gates,
Ye everlasting Doors give Way.

Loose all your Bars of massy Light,
And wide unfold th' etherial Scene;
He claims those Mansions as his Right,
Receive the King of Glory in!

Who is the King of Glory, who?
The Lord that all his Foes o'ercame;
The World, Sin, Death, and Hell o'erthrew,
And Jesus is the Conqu'ror's Name.

Lo! his triumphal Chariot waits,
And Angels chant the solemn Lay,
Lift up your Heads, ye heav'nly Gates,
Ye everlasting Doors give Way!

Who is the King of Glory, who?
The Lord of glorious Pow'r possest,
The King of Saints and Angels too,
God over all, for ever blest!

HYMN CXI. For Whitsunday.

GRANTED is the SAVIOUR's Prayer,
  Now descends the COMFORTER;
Open wide your Hearts to prove,
All the Powers of Life and Love.

Come, divine and peaceful Guest,
Enter now each waiting Breast;
Holy Ghost our Hearts inspire,
Kindle there the Gospel-Fire.

Crown the agonizing Strife,
Principle and LORD of Life,
Life divine in us renew,
Thou the Gift and Giver too.

Now descend and shake the Earth,
Wake us into second Birth:
Now thy quickning Influence give,
Breathe, and these dry Bones shall live.

Bid our Sin and Sorrow cease,
Fill us with thine heav'nly Peace;
Joy divine we then shall prove,
Light of Truth, and Fire of Love.

HYMN CXII. *The same.*

JESU, we hang upon the Word
  Our longing Souls have heard from Thee,
Be mindful of thy Promise, LORD!
  Thy Promise made to all, and me,
Thy Foll'wers who thy Steps pursue,
And dare believe that GOD is true.

Thou saidst, I will the Father pray,
   And He the PARACLETE shall give,
Shall give Him in your Hearts to stay,
   And never more his Temples leave;
Myself will to my Orphans come,
And make you mine eternal Home.

Come then, dear LORD! Thyself reveal,
   And let the Promise now take Place!
Be it according to thy Will,
   According to the Word of Grace!
Thy sorrowful Disciples chear,
And send us down the COMFORTER!

He visits now the troubled Breast,
   And oft relieves our sad Complaint;
But soon we lose the transient Guest;
   But soon we droop again, and faint,
Repeat the melancholy Moan—
" Our Joy is fled, our Comfort gone!"

Hasten Him, LORD, into each Heart,
   Our sure inseparable Guide——
O might we meet, and never part!
   O might He in our Hearts abide!
And keep his House of Praise and Pray'r,
And rest, and reign for ever—There!

HYMN CXIII. To the TRINITY.

BLESS'D be the Father, and his Love,
   To whose celestial Source we owe
Rivers of endless Joys above,
And Rills of Comfort here below.

Glory to Thee, great Son of God,
From whose dear wounded Body rolls
A precious Stream of vital Blood,
Pardon and Life for dying Souls.

We give the sacred SPIRIT Praise,
Who in our Hearts of Sin and Woe,
Makes living Springs of Grace arise,
And into boundless Glory flow.

Thus GOD the FATHER, GOD the SON,
And GOD the SPIRIT we adore,
That Sea of Life and Love unknown,
Without a Bottom or a Shore.

HYMN CXIV. *The same.*

COME, Thou Almighty King,
  Help us thy Name to sing,
    Help us to praise!
FATHER all-glorious,
O'er all victorious!
Come and reign over us,
    ANTIENT OF DAYS.

JESUS, our LORD, arise,
Scatter our Enemies,
    And make them fall!
Let thine Almighty Aid
Our sure Defence be made,
Our Souls on Thee be stay'd;
    LORD, hear our Call.

Come, Thou Incarnate WORD,
Gird on thy mighty Sword——
    Our Pray'r attend!

Come! and thy People bless,
And give thy Word Success,
Spirit of Holiness,
On us descend!

Come, Holy Comforter,
Thy sacred Witness bear
In this glad Hour!
Thou who Almighty art,
Now rule in ev'ry Heart,
And ne'er from us depart,
Spirit of Power!

To the Great One in Three
Eternal Praises be
Hence—Evermore!
His Sov'reign Majesty
May we in Glory see,
And to Eternity
Love and adore!

HYMN CXV. *The same.*

HAIL, holy, holy, holy Lord!
Be endless Praise to Thee;
Supreme, essential One ador'd,
In co-eternal Three!

Enthron'd in everlasting State,
Ere Time its Round began,
Who join'd in Council to create
The Dignity of Man.

All that the Name of Creature owns,
To Thee in Hymns aspire;
May we as Angels on our Thrones
For ever join the Choir!

HYMN CXVI. *The same.*

WE give immortal Praise
    To God the Father's Love:
For all our Comforts here,
  And better Hopes above:
He sent his own eternal Son,
To die for Sins that Man had done.

  To God the Son belongs
    Immortal Glory too,
  Who bought us with his Blood,
    From everlasting Woe.
And now He lives, and now He reigns,
And sees the Fruit of all his Pains.

  To God the Spirit's Name,
    Immortal Worship give;
  Whose new-creating Pow'r
    Makes the dead Sinner live.
His Work compleats the great Design,
And fills the Soul with Joy divine.

  Almighty God to Thee
    Be endless Honours done;
  The undivided Three,
    And the mysterious One!
Where Reason fails with all her Pow'rs,
There Faith prevails, and Love adores.

FUNERAL HYMNS.

HYMN CXVII.

WHY should we mourn departing Friends,
    Or shake at Death's Alarms?
'Tis but the Voice that Jesus sends
  To call them to his Arms.

Are we not tending upward too,
　As fast as Time can move?
Why should we wish the Hours more slow,
　That keep us from our Love?

Why should we tremble to convey
　Their Bodies to the Tomb?
There the dear Flesh of Jesus lay,
　And left a sweet Perfume.

The Graves of all his Saints he bless'd,
　And soften'd every Bed:
Where should the dying Members rest,
　But with their dying Head?

Thence He arose, ascending high,
　And shew'd our Feet the Way;
Up to the Lord our Flesh shall fly
　At the great rising Day.

HYMN CXVIII. *The same.*

MY Soul, come meditate the Day,
　And think how near it stands,
When thou must quit this House of Clay,
　And fly to unknown Lands.

O could we die with those that die,
　And place us in their Stead!
Then would our Spirits learn to fly,
　And converse with the Dead.

Then should we see the Saints above
　In their own glorious Forms,
And wonder why our Souls should love
　To dwell with mortal Worms.

HYMN CXIX. The Last Judgment.

LO! He comes with Clouds descending,
  Once for favour'd Sinners slain!
Thousand thousand Saints attending,
Swell the Triumph of his Train:
    Hallelujah!
    Hallelujah! Amen.

Ev'ry Eye shall now behold Him,
  Rob'd in dreadful Majesty;
Those who set at nought and sold Him,
  Pierc'd and nail'd Him to the Tree,
    Deeply wailing,
  Shall the true MESSIAH see.

Ev'ry Island, Sea, and Mountain,
  Heav'n and Earth shall flee away;
All who hate Him, must confounded
  Hear the Trump proclaim the Day;
    Come to Judgment!
  Come to Judgment! come away!

Now Redemption long expected,
  See! in solemn Pomp appear!
All his Saints by Man rejected,
  Now shall meet Him in the Air!
    Hallelujah!
  See the Day of GOD appear!

Answer thine own Bride and Spirit,
  Hasten, LORD, the gen'ral Doom!
The new Heav'n and Earth t' inherit,
  Take thy pining Exiles Home:
    All Creation
  Travails! groans! and bids Thee come!

Yea! Amen! Let all adore Thee,
  High on thine eternal Throne!
Saviour, take the Pow'r and Glory:
  Claim the Kingdom for thine own!
    O come quickly,
      Hallelujah! Come, LORD, come!

HYMN CXX. *The same.*

HE comes! He comes! the Judge severe!
  The seventh Trumpet speaks him near:
His Lightnings flash, his Thunders roll,
He's welcome to the faithful Soul;
Welcome, welcome, welcome, welcome, welcome to the faithful Soul.

From Heav'n, angelic Voices sound,
  See the Almighty JESUS crown'd!
Girt with Omnipotence and Grace,
And Glory decks the Saviour's Face,
Glory, Glory, Glory, Glory, Glory, &c.

Descending on his Azure Throne,
  He claims the Kingdoms for his own:
The Kingdoms all obey his Word,
And hail Him their triumphant LORD:
Hail Him, Hail Him, Hail Him, &c.

Shout all the People of the Sky,
  And all the Saints of the Most High:
Our GOD, who now his Right obtains,
  For ever and for ever reigns:
Ever, ever, ever, ever, ever, &c.

The Father praise, the Son adore,
The Spirit bless for evermore:
Salvation's glorious Work is done,
We welcome Thee great Three in One!
Welcome, welcome Thee great Three in One.

HYMN CXXI.

For Persons join'd in Fellowship.

JESUS, Lord, we look to Thee,
   Let us in thy Name agree,
Shew thyself the Prince of Peace,
Bid our Jars for ever cease.

By thy reconciling Love,
Every Stumbling-Block remove,
Each to each unite, endear,
Come and spread thy Banner here.

Make us of one Heart and Mind,
Courteous, pitiful, and kind,
Lowly, meek in Thought and Word,
Altogether like our Lord.

Let us each for other care,
Each his Brother's Burden bear,
To thy Church the Pattern give,
Shew how true Believers live.

Let us then with Joy remove
To thy Family above,
On the Wings of Angels fly,
Shew how true Believers die.

HYMN CXXII. *The same.*

JESUS attend, Thyself reveal,
  Are we not met in thy great Name!
Thee in the Midst we wait to feel,
  We wait to catch the spreading Flame.

Thou GOD that answerest by Fire,
  The Spirit of Burning now impart!
And let the Flames of pure Desire
  Rise from the Altar of each Heart!

Truly our Fellowship below,
  With Thee, and with thy Father is,
In Thee eternal Life we know,
  And Heav'n's unutterable Bliss!

In Part we only know Thee here,
  But wait thy Coming from above,
Then shall we, LORD, behold Thee near,
  And we shall all be lost in Love.

HYMN CXXIII. At Meeting.

BLEST by JESU's Providence,
  Lo! we meet again in Peace!
May we, when we fly from hence,
  Meet in a more glorious Place!

When we once shall there arrive,
  Ever happy we shall reign;
Ever with our Saviour live,
  'Midst a Host of perfect Men.

There shall Sorrow not intrude,
  Grief shall never there appear:
Wash'd in our Redeemer's Blood,
  We shall stand made free from Fear.

Come, dear Fellows, joyful, come,
Forward boldly let us prefs,
Humbly let our Souls prefume,
Truft in JESU's Righteoufnefs.

Pray we for the promis'd Hour,
When the Family compleat,
Borne on Clouds, and girt with Pow'r,
In the Houfe above fhall meet.

Mafter, haften on thy Day!
Glorious to thy Judgment come!
Call thy trav'ling Saints away;
LORD, we long to be at Home.

HYMN CXXIV. At Parting.

BLEST be the dear uniting Love,
   That will not let us part;
Our Bodies may far off remove,
   We ftill are join'd in Heart.

Join'd in one Spirit to our Head,
   Where He appoints we go,
And ftill in JESU's Footfteps tread,
   And do his Work below.

O let us ever walk in Him,
   And nothing know befide,
Nothing defire, nothing efteem,
   But JESUS crucify'd.

Clofer and clofer let us cleave
   To his belov'd Embrace,
Expect his Fulnefs to receive,
   And Grace to anfwer Grace.

F

Thus let us hasten to the Day,
   Which shall our Flesh restore,
When Death shall all be done away,
   And Bodies part no more.

HYMN CXXV.
For Ministers at Meeting.

WELCOME, welcome, blessed Servant,
   Messenger of JESU's Grace!
O how beautiful the Feet of
Him that brings good News of Peace?
   All hail, Herald, &c.
   Priest of GOD, thy People's Joy.

SAVIOUR, bless his Message to us,
Give us Hearts to hear the Sound
Of Redemption, dearly purchas'd
By thy Death and precious Wounds.
   O reveal it, &c.
   To our poor and helpless Souls.

Give Reward of Grace and Glory,
To thy faithful Labourer dear,
Let the Incense of our Hearts be
Offer'd up in Faith and Prayer.
   Bless, O bless him, &c.
   Now, henceforth, for evermore.

HYMN CXXVI.
For Ministers at Parting.

WITH all thy Pow'r, O LORD, defend
   Him whom we now to Thee commend;
Our faithful Minister secure,
And make him to the End endure.

Gird him with all-sufficient Grace;
Give to his Footsteps Paths of Peace;
Thy Truth and Faithfulness fulfil,
Preserve him, LORD, from ev'ry Ill.

Before his Face Protection send;
O love him, save him to the End!
Nor let him as thy Pilgrim rove,
Without the Convoy of thy Love.

Enlarge, enflame, and fill his Heart,
In him thy mighty Power exert;
That Thousands yet unborn may praise
The Wonders of redeeming Grace.

HYMN CXXVII. *Infant-Baptism.*

THUS did the Sons of Abr'am pass
 Under the bloody Seal of Grace:
The young Disciples bore the Yoke,
Till CHRIST the painful Bondage broke.

By milder Ways doth JESUS prove
His Father's Cov'nant and his Love:
He seals to Saints his glorious Grace;
And not forbids their Infant-Race.

Their Seed is sprinkled with his Blood;
Their Children set apart for GOD;
His Spirit on their Offspring shed,
Like Water pour'd upon the Head.

Let ev'ry Saint with chearful Voice
In this large Covenant rejoice;
Young Children in their early Days,
Shall give the GOD of Abr'am Praise.

HYMN CXXVIII. Adult-Baptism.

Descend, celestial Dove!
 In ev'ry Bosom dwell;
Upon the present Water move
 While we the Influence feel.

Anoint with holy Fire,
 Baptize with purging Flames
This Soul, and with thy Grace inspire,
 In ceaseless living Streams.

Thy heav'nly Unction give;
 Thy Promise, Lord, fulfil;
Give Pow'r thy Spirit to receive,
 And Strength to do thy Will.

Thy Ord'nance we obey,
 O meet us in the same;
And with this Water now convey
 The Virtues of thy Name.

Witness to this thy Sign,
 And grant the inward Grace;
Let this thy Servant seal'd for thine,
 From hence depart in Peace.

SACRAMENTAL HYMNS.

HYMN CXXIX.

Lamb of God, whose bleeding Love
 We thus recal to mind,
Send the Answer from above,
 And let us Mercy find;

Think on us, who think on Thee,
  And ev'ry ſtruggling Soul releaſe;
O remember Calvary,
  And bid us go in Peace.

By thine agonizing Pain,
  And bloody Sweat, we pray;
By thy dying Love to Man,
  Take all our Sins away:
Burſt our Bonds, and ſet us free,
  From all Iniquity releaſe;
O remember Calvary,
  And bid us go in Peace.

Let thy Blood, by Faith apply'd,
  The Sinner's Pardon feal,
Speak us freely juſtify'd,
  And all our Sickneſs heal:
By thy Paſſion on the Tree,
  Let all our Griefs and Troubles ceaſe:
O remember Calvary,
  And bid us go in Peace.

Never let us hence depart,
  Till Thou our Wants relieve:
Write Forgiveneſs in our Heart,
  And all thine Image give:
May our Souls ſtill cry to Thee,
  Till perfected in Holineſs;
O remember Calvary,
  And bid us go in Peace.

The Lords Supper institute
1 Cor. 11.23 Pet.

HYMN CXXX.

'TWAS on that dark, that doleful Night,
  When Pow'rs of Earth and Hell arose
Against the Son of God's Delight,
And Friends betray'd Him to his Foes:

Before the mournful Scene began,
He took the Bread, and bless'd, and brake;
What Love thro' all his Actions ran!
What wond'rous Words of Grace He spake!

" This is my Body broke for Sin,
" Receive and eat the living Food."
Then took the Cup, and bless'd the Wine!
" This the New Cov'nant in my Blood.

" Do this," he cry'd, " till Time shall end,
" In Mem'ry of your dying Friend;
" Meet at my Table, and record
" The Love of your departed Lord."

JESUS, thy Feast we celebrate,
We shew thy Death, we sing thy Name,
Till Thou return, and we shall eat
The Marriage-Supper of the LAMB.

HYMN CXXXI.

THANKFUL for our ev'ry Blessing
    Let us sing,
    CHRIST the Spring,
Never, never ceasing.

Source of all our Gifts and Graces,
    CHRIST we own,
    CHRIST alone
Calls for all our Praises.

He dispels our Sin and Sadness,
    Life imparts,
    Chears our Hearts,
Fills with Food and Gladness.

He Himself for us hath given,
    Us He feeds,
    Us He leads
To a Feast in Heav'n.

HYMN CXXXII.

ALAS! and did our Saviour bleed?
  And did our Sov'reign die?
Would he devote that sacred Head
  For such a Worm as I?

Was it for Crimes that I had done,
  He groan'd upon the Tree?
Amazing Pity! Grace unknown,
  And Love beyond Degree!

Well might the Sun in Darkness hide,
  And shut his Glories in,
When God the mighty Maker dy'd
  For Man the Creature's Sin.

Thus might I hide my blushing Face,
  While his dear Cross appears;
Dissolve my Heart in Thankfulness,
  And melt my Eyes to Tears.

But Drops of Grief can ne'er repay,
  The Debt of Love I owe;
May I here give myself away!
  'Tis all that I can do.

HYMN CXXXIII.

WHEN Saints survey the wondrous Cross
   On which the Prince of Glory dy'd,
Their richest Gain they count but Loss,
And pour Contempt on all their Pride.

Forbid it, LORD, that they should boast,
Save in the Death of CHRIST, their GOD;
All the vain Things that charm them most,
They sacrifice them to his Blood.

See from his Head, his Hands, his Feet,
Sorrow and Love flow mingled down!
Did e'er such Love and Sorrow meet,
Or Thorns compose so rich a Crown?

Were the whole Realm of Nature mine,
That were a Present far too small:
Love so amazing, so divine,
Demands my Soul, my Life, my All.

HYMN CXXXIV.

LOVE brought down GOD's dear only Son
   Into a Virgin's Womb,
Love nail'd Him to th' accursed Tree,
   And laid Him in a Tomb.

Through ev'ry Action, suff'ring too,
   The Law of Kindness reign'd,
Love op'd those ghastly Wounds thro' which
   His precious Life was drain'd.

Love took him to his Father's Throne,
   There to prepare us Room,
And Love will bring Him down again,
   To fetch us to his Home.

HYMN CXXXV.

OF Him who did Salvation bring,
   Lord, may we ever think and sing!
Arise, ye Guilty, he'll forgive;
Arise, ye Needy, he'll relieve.

Eternal Lord, Almighty King,
All Heav'n doth with thy Triumphs ring!
Thou conquer'st all beneath, above,
Devils with Force, and Men with Love!

To purge our Sins, Christ shed his Blood,
He dy'd to bring us near to God:
Let all the World fall down and know,
That none but God such Love could show.

HYMN CXXXVI.

HAPPY the Man to whom 'tis given
   To eat the Bread of Life in Heav'n;
This Happiness in Christ they prove,
Who feed on his forgiving Love.

HYMN CXXXVII.

COME, Holy Ghost, set to thy Seal,
   Thine inward Witness give,
To all our waiting Souls reveal
   The Death by which we live.

Spectators of the Pangs divine,
   O that we now may be;
Discerning in the sacred Sign,
   His Passion on the Tree:

Repeat the Saviour's dying Cry
 In ev'ry Heart so loud,
That ev'ry Heart may now reply,
 " This was the Son of God!"

HYMN CXXXVIII.

LAMB of God, for whom we languish,
 Make thy Grief our Relief;
Ease us by thine Anguish!

O our agonizing Saviour!
 By thy Pain, let us gain
God's eternal Favour!

In thine own Appointment bless us;
 Meet us here, now appear
Our Almighty Jesus!

Let the Ordinance be sealing;
 Enter now, claim us Thou
For thy constant Dwelling.

Fill the Heart of each Believer:
 We are Thine, Love divine,
Reign in us for ever.

HYMN CXXXIX.

JESUS invites his Saints
 To meet around his Board!
Here pardon'd Rebels sit, and hold
 Communion with their Lord.

For Food He gives his Flesh:
 He bids us drink his Blood:
Amazing Favour! Matchless Grace
 Of our redeeming God!

Let all our Pow'rs be join'd
His glorious Name to raise!
Pleasure and Love fill ev'ry Mind,
And ev'ry Voice be Praise.

HYMN CXL.

ALL Praise to the LORD, all Praise is his Due,
To-day is his Word of Promise found true;
We, we are the Nations presented to GOD,
Well-pleasing Oblations thro' JESUS's Blood.

Poor Gentiles from far to JESUS we came,
And offer'd we are to GOD thro' his Name;
To GOD thro' the Spirit ourselves may we give,
While fav'd by the Merit of JESUS we live.

HYMN CXLI.

WHAT Creatures beside
   Are favour'd like us?
Forgiven, supplied,
   And banquetted thus
By GOD our good Father;
   Who gave us his Son,
And sent Him to gather
   His Children in One?

Salvation's of GOD,
   Th' Effect of free Grace,
Upon us bestow'd
   Before the World was.
GOD from Everlasting
   Be blest; and again
Blest to Everlasting;
   Amen, and Amen.

HYMN CXLII.

O Love divine, what haſt thou done!
   Th' immortal GOD hath dy'd for me:
The Father's co-eternal Son
   Bore all my Sins upon the Tree:
Th' immortal GOD for me hath dy'd;
My LORD, my Love, is crucify'd!

Behold Him, all ye that paſs by
   The bleeding Prince of Life and Peace!
Come, ſee, ye Worms, your Maker die,
   And ſay, " Was ever Grief like His!"
Come, feel with me his Blood apply'd,
My LORD, my Love, is crucify'd!

Is crucify'd for me and you,
   To bring us Rebels back to GOD:
Believe, and feel the Record true,
   That we are bought with JESU's Blood;
Pardon and Life flow from his Side:
My LORD, my Love, is crucify'd!

Then let us ſit beneath his Croſs,
   And gladly catch the healing Stream!
All Things for him account but Loſs,
   And give up all our Hearts to Him;
Of nothing ſpeak or think beſide:
My LORD, my Love, is crucify'd!

N. B. *See Hymns on the* CRUCIFIXION.

DISMISSION HYMNS.

HYMN CXLIII.

LORD, dismiss us with thy Blessing;
  Fill our Hearts with Joy and Peace;
Let us each, thy Love possessing,
  Triumph in redeeming Grace:
    O refresh us, &c.
  Trav'ling thro' this Wilderness.

Thanks we give and Adoration
  For thy Gospel's joyful Sound:
May the Fruits of thy Salvation
  In our Hearts and Lives abound!
    Ever faithful, &c.
  To the Truth may we be found!

So whene'er the Signal's given
  Us from Earth to call away,
Borne on Angel's Wing to Heaven,
  Glad the Summons to obey,
    May we ever, &c.
  Reign with CHRIST in endless Day!

HYMN CXLIV.

THIS GOD is the GOD we adore,
  Our faithful unchangeable Friend:
Whose Love is as great as his Pow'r,
And neither knows Measure nor End.

'Tis Jesus, the First and the Last;
Whose Spirit shall guide us safe Home:
We'll praise Him for all that is past,
And trust Him for all that's to come.

HYMN CXLV.

NO farther go to Night, but stay,
   Dear Saviour, till the Break of Day;
Turn in, dear Lord, with me:
And in the Morning when I wake,
Me in thine Arms, my Jesus, take,
   And I'll go on with Thee.

HYMN CXLVI.

DISMISS us with thy Blessing, Lord;
   Help us to feed upon thy Word:
All that has been amiss forgive,
And let thy Truth within us live.

Tho' we are guilty, Thou art good;
Wash all our Works in Jesu's Blood;
Give ev'ry fetter'd Soul Release,
And bid us all depart in Peace.

HYMN CXLVII.

IF Jesus is ours we have a true Friend,
   His Goodness endures the same to the End:
Our Tempers may vary, our Comforts decline,
We cannot miscarry, our Aid is divine.

HYMN CXLVIII.

NONE but Jesus will we sing,
   None else will we adore;
He our Prophet, Priest, and King,
   Shall be for evermore.
None among the heav'nly Pow'rs,
   Nor one on Earth, our Praise may claim;
None but Jesus call we ours;
   None but the bleeding Lamb!

DOXOLOGIES.

PRAISE God, from whom all Blessings flow;
   Praise Him, all Creatures here below;
Praise Him above, ye heav'nly Host;
Praise Father, Son, and Holy Ghost.

TO Father, Son, and Holy Ghost,
   One God, whom we adore,
Be Glory; as it was, is now,
   And shall be evermore.

FATHER, Son, and Holy Ghost,
   One God whom we adore,
Join we with the heav'nly Host,
   To praise Thee evermore.
Live by Heav'n and Earth ador'd,
Three in One and One in Three;
Holy, holy, holy Lord,
   All Glory be to Thee.

SING we to our God above,
   Praise, eternal as his Love:
Praise Him, all ye heav'nly Host,
Praise Father, Son, and Holy Ghost.

TO God, who reigns enthron'd on high,
    To his dear Son, who deign'd to die,
Our Guilt and Curse t' remove,
To that blest Spirit who Life imparts,
Who rules in all believing Hearts;
    Be endless Glory, Praise and Love.

TO Father, Son, and Holy Ghost,
    Be Praise amidst the heav'nly Host,
And in the Church below;
From whom all Creatures drew their Birth,
By whom Redemption blest the Earth,
    From whom all Comforts flow.

GIVE to the Father Praise,
    Give Glory to the Son,
And to the Spirit of his Grace
    Be equal Honours done.

TO God the Father's Throne,
    Perpetual Honours raise:
Glory to God the Son,
To God the Spirit Praise:
    With all our Pow'rs,
    Eternal King,
    Thy Name we sing,
    While Faith adores.

GIVE Glory to God, ye Children of Men;
    And publish abroad again and again
The Son's glorious Merit, the Father's free Grace,
The Gifts of the Spirit, to Adam's lost Race.

      FINIS.

www.ingramcontent.com/pod-product-compliance
Lightning Source LLC
Chambersburg PA
CBHW020137170426
43199CB00010B/779